OVERCOME
BY THE *S PIRIT*

Ein Methodist Campmeeting.

Courtesy of Billy Graham Center Museum, Wheaton College, Wheaton, IL 60187

OVERCOME

BY THE SPIRIT

FRANCIS MacNUTT

Chosen Books

A Division of Baker Book House Co
Grand Rapids, Michigan 49516

Library of Congress Cataloging-in-Publication Data

MacNutt, Francis.
    Overcome by the Spirit / Francis MacNutt.
      p. cm.
    Includes bibliographical references.
    ISBN 0-8007-9170-3
    1. Slain in the Spirit.   I. Title.
BT123.M153   1990
248.2′9—dc20
                                  90-44727
                                    CIP

Sixth printing, June 1998

Printed in the United States of America

To Judith
and
Rachel and David

Contents

OVERCOME BY THE *SPIRIT*

Part I

The Phenomenon of Resting in the Spirit

Introduction: Why This Book Was Written

Why write a book on such a controversial topic as people falling to the ground when they are prayed for? After all, most Christians in mainline churches have never even heard of this phenomenon, much less witnessed it.

There are several reasons, nevertheless, why I feel such a book is important—even necessary—at this time. The Pentecostal movement worldwide is growing at an extraordinary rate, and the falling phenomenon, which accompanies the Pentecostal explosion, is also on the increase. Already in the charismatic renewal and in the so-called Third Wave, tens of thousands of mainline church members have had this experience and are wondering what it all means. Father Ralph DiOrio, for instance, conducts healing services attended by thousands of people, mostly Catholics; when he prays, many of them fall in the aisles.

And although Pentecostals have been familiar for generations with being "slain in the Spirit" (as they term it), they have not spent much time reflecting on its meaning; they simply accept it as a demonstration of God's power. I believe that resting in the Spirit has a very wonderful additional purpose that I am eager to share with you.

When people fall over in a church service it does attract attention, and authorities are forced to say something about it. The increasingly frequent appearance of this phenomenon in mainline denominations has provoked a predictable cautionary reaction. Cardinal Suenens, for example, an influential spokesman for charismatic renewal in the Roman Catholic Church, is concerned that people will be misled into desiring sensational experiences that may well be psychological aberrations rather than genuine touches of the Spirit of God.

Father Theodore Dobson, too, wonders how we can be sure the Holy Spirit is behind such "fallings." Might they not be caused by mass suggestion or autohypnosis? Dobson writes, "Rev. George Maloney wants to know what psychologists, especially those who have studied religious phenomena, would have to say about the workings of the psyche under the influence of religious enthusiasm. . . . He wants to hear the comments of psychologists on the role of crowd psychology in a religious service in which verbal suggestibility is backed up with physical suggestion as people are seen to be falling to the ground in front of the entire congregation."[1]

These are legitimate concerns; there can be very natural and human reasons causing people to fall over. For some in positions of responsibility, such fears render the entire phenomenon suspect—as in this recent statement put out by the leadership of the Roman Catholic charismatic renewal in Ireland:

Pastorally, we suggest:

a) that the term "slaying in the Spirit" should at all times be avoided as this inclines people immediately to the discernment that it is, or may very likely be, from God. We think it is far better to follow the Rev. John Richards in adopting the neutral term "falling." That accurately describes what happens and leads to a more objective and unprejudiced discernment as to why they have fallen.

b) we would always discourage circumstances in which the phenomenon would occur.

c) we would not invite ministers whose prayer or teaching is associated with this phenomenon.

d) in speaking about "slaying in the Spirit," we would always adopt a negative approach, leaving open the possibility, however, that on some very few occasions this may be a gift from God.[2]

In the face of these doubts about the validity of what I see, in general, as an authentic gift from God, I want to share what I believe are the ordinary benefits of "resting in the Spirit"—my preferred term. I would like to turn the statement of the Irish leaders on its head and say, "In speaking about 'slaying in the Spirit,' we would ordinarily adopt a positive approach, leaving open the possibility, however, that on some few occasions this may not be a gift, but a problematic occurrence."

Here I speak from some 22 years of experience in the healing ministry, with eighteen years of experience since I first noticed people slumping over while I was praying for them. Firsthand I have encountered all of the problems described by the critics, but believe these problems are far outweighed by the wonderful blessings and healings I have seen take place while people were resting peacefully.

One fascinating paradox is that, although theologians and church leaders are generally critical of the falling phenomenon and call for psychologists to investigate what is going on, the two most positive books I have read on the subject are by Dr. John White, a *psychiatrist* who has followed and studied John Wimber's ministry, and Dr. David Lewis, a *social anthropologist* who undertook a comprehensive analysis of Wimber's 1986 Harrogate conference in England. Both scientists are basically positive about the extraordinary happenings they have witnessed, including "slaying in the Spirit" (which Dr. White himself experienced). White writes,

> My main theme has to do with the church's panicky flight at the approach of revival, and the failure to recognize it when God sends it. Revival has dangers. But our fear may lead us to reject what God sends. We must not neglect power because it has dangers.
>
> The greatest fear in some quarters is that what appears to be the power of God may be nothing more than a massive hoax by the enemy. It is a fear that is paralyzing whole segments of the church, a dread that debilitates, that causes our hands to hang slack and our feet to lag at a time when the trumpet calls for advance and attack.[3]

So here we have a paradox, a sign of the times: Church leaders warning ministers of healing to stay away from anything that might lead people to fall over, for fear that the falling phenomenon may be purely psychological, and calling on psychologists to see if that isn't so; and on the other hand, a psychiatrist and an anthropologist observing that the Church is fearful and excessively influenced by the Western, scientific, rationalistic worldview of our culture! Religion calling on science to warn people; science calling on religion to trust more in God and loosen up!

In this book I want to share what I have learned through praying with thousands of people and talking with them afterwards. What really does happen to people? And does it help?

A Note to the Reader
Much of what I write in this book presupposes a familiarity with such charismatic concepts as healing through prayer, deliverance from evil spirits, praying in tongues and the baptism in the Spirit. If you would like to learn more about these elements in what I believe should be ordinary Christian experience, you might turn to the brief bibliography in the back of this book.

1
My Own Experience

The first time I saw someone slain in the Spirit was in 1970.

I had heard a great deal about this curious phenomenon, about how people were touched by ministers who had this gift and just toppled over "under the power." I had talked to one priest who had been to a Kathryn Kuhlman meeting in Pittsburgh and was so sensitive to this power that he couldn't even get near her but repeatedly fell down in the aisle as he tried to approach the platform. It sounded weird. What was the purpose of it? It all seemed very circus-like; it also seemed to demean human dignity, and I questioned whether this was a way God would act.

But when I finally went to a Kathryn Kuhlman meeting, I was struck by the effect of slaying in the Spirit (as she called it) upon the crowd: It led them to glorify God's power. Rather than demeaning people, it seemed as if a real blessing was being imparted, a blessing so powerful that people's bodies were not able to contain it. Too, I had a chance to talk to several people who had actually been slain in the Spirit. They reported that they felt as light as a feather when they fell; then, during the period when they lay on the floor, they experienced great peace and a sense of God's presence. That softened me up a bit; maybe being slain was worthwhile if it brought a real interior blessing and was not merely a flashy gimmick that some evangelists used to excite the crowd.

So, when someone spotted me in the crowd and an usher brought me up onto the platform, I welcomed the opportunity to be prayed for by Miss Kuhlman. If Jesus wanted to bless me in some deep interior way, I didn't want to resist; I wanted to receive God's blessing, however it might come.

As Kathryn approached me I stood determined not to fight it, whatever it was. A "catcher" stood behind me while several thousand people watched. I felt the gentle pressure of Kathryn's hand on my forehead. I had to make a decision; if I didn't take a step backward, her hand's pressure would push me off-balance and I would fall. *But,* I thought to myself, *I don't want to resist in any way if this is from God.*

So I didn't step back and, sure enough, I fell—all six feet four inches of me. The crowd made a noise, a combination of surprise and delight at seeing a priest in a Roman collar topple over on the stage.

Then I quickly scrambled to my feet, not sure that I hadn't been pushed. Again Kathryn prayed; again I felt pressure on my forehead that I did not resist. Once more I fell.

It was confusing. Others, I knew, had experienced something remarkable. But if I had only my own experience to go on, I would have judged that nothing in particular had happened—that I might simply have been pushed off-balance. I didn't know what to make of it.

In time, though, and almost imperceptibly, I began to see it happen right in front of me as I prayed for others. At first it happened only when I was helping someone else pray. I remember, for instance (in 1971 I think it was), praying with the Rev. Tommy Tyson for an older man seated on a chair. This man acted as though he had fallen asleep and almost fell off that chair. I remember being surprised that Tommy was not surprised! Nor did he appear worried that the man might have suffered a heart attack.

Perhaps a year later, a few people I was praying for started to experience something similar in a very mild way. Since I usually prayed for people who were sitting down, all I had to do to prevent them from slumping in their seats was to stop praying.

Those times, then, when I noticed something strange going on, I would stop praying before anything startling happened. I saw no point in leading people to look for extraordinary experiences and distracting onlookers. (We had enough problems as it was with critics of the healing ministry!) If people blacked out, I figured it would inhibit anything in the spiritual order that God might want to accomplish. After all, all that I'd seen thus far in evangelists' meetings was people falling over and getting immediately to their feet. The rapidity with which all this took place, the carnival atmosphere, hardly led to the impression that anything deep was going on within people's spirits.

But then several people I prayed for fell back and proceeded to rest for a considerable period of time.

Afterwards they told me of some deep spiritual experiences they had had while in this state. I began to wonder if this phenomenon was related in any way to the "ecstasy" mentioned in the lives of the mystics of the Church, in which the intensity of a spiritual experience was so great that the senses and body were temporarily incapacitated, as in the apostle Paul's celebrated experience:

> I know a man in Christ who fourteen years ago was caught up to the third heaven. Whether it was in the body or out of the body I do not know—God knows. And I know that this man—whether in the body or apart from the body I do not know, but God knows— was caught up to Paradise. He heard inexpressible things, things that man is not permitted to tell.
>
> 2 Corinthians 12:2–4

By happy coincidence Judith (later my wife) saw the same thing happen in her ministry in the mid-1970s, before we even knew each other. At a retreat in Lantana, Florida, she was praying for a woman who had asked for the healing of her heart condition. While Judith prayed the woman slid off the chair and fell to the floor. Judith was afraid the lady had suffered a heart attack then and there! Then she noticed that the woman was smiling, and when Judith checked her pulse and her breathing, she found they were normal. In a little while the woman sat up; she had been healed!

I began to encounter the falling phenomenon with increasing frequency. I remember praying for about fifteen people, for instance, after a Mass on Pentecost Sunday at a conference in Arkansas. People seemed a little groggy during the prayer and several of them fell to the floor.

Another time, following a powerful prayer by friends in Clearwater, Florida, asking that I might receive God's increased help in ministry, I traveled to Washington, D.C., for one of the rallies of "Jesus '73." There Barbara Shlemon and I prayed for healing as a team at National Presbyterian Church. This time everyone we prayed for, except one man, promptly fell down. Since that time it has happened regularly. So I had to try to understand what it was all about in order to know whether I should

- *Encourage* it;

- Try to *ignore* it;

- Or try to *prevent* its happening.

After talking to many people who had had the experience, I decided it was usually a helpful state to be in: Healing seemed more likely to occur when people were resting in this way. I started talking about it before healing services began, so that people would not be frightened but would understand how it might help them.

Then in 1977 I wrote a chapter on "Resting in the Spirit" in my book *The Power to Heal.* I still believe what I stated there: that the best way to judge the value of this experience is by checking with the people to whom it happens.

Not surprisingly, questions and opposition followed. Some of the outstanding leaders in charismatic renewal warned against healing ministers' inducing people to fall, as if *we were doing something* to bring it about. Cardinal Suenens, for instance, wrote:

The most influential propagandist during the seventies was the ex-Dominican priest Francis Mac-Nutt. . . .

A few years ago, I personally took part in a seminar for psychiatrists and moralists, held by Francis Mac-Nutt in Florida. On that occasion, I attended "slain in the Spirit" sessions where people would line up before him to receive laying on of hands, then fall to the ground one after the other.[1]

(This particular meeting, held in Tampa in 1975, was the inaugural conference of the Association of Christian Therapists, a group of healing professionals now numbering 2,000 members—doctors, nurses, counselors, social workers and clergy—hardly an unsophisticated gathering who would line up to submit uncritically to a sensationalist demonstration.)

These perceptions—that *we* were doing this to people and that we were conducting "slain in the Spirit" sessions—have been a misunderstanding from the beginning. We were conducting healing sessions, during which some people rested in the Spirit. What we were, in fact, praying for was blessing or healing, not that people be slain in the Spirit. Most of the people I know (including Judith and myself) who find that people "rest" in their ministry discovered this phenomenon by accident and were amazed the first time it happened. It certainly wasn't anything we induced.

The opposition I encountered, interestingly, was seldom expressed by people to whom the experience had occurred. Opposition came from those who observed, as it were, from the back of the hall. And because so much good seemed to come to people who rested, I concluded that I should not try to prevent its happening. It seemed to me that God was doing something to help us as we attempted to minister to hundreds of sick people; I didn't want to block His healing power by being over-cautious.

What Do We Call It?

One of the difficulties in communicating about this subject—as has already become clear!—is the matter of terminology. What we call the experience determines in large measure how we relate to it.

What we see, from outside, is people falling over. What happens inside the person—if anything—we can't see. The Pentecostals, who were the first people I ever heard talking about this experience (Kathryn Kuhlman, for example), called this spectacular phenomenon being *slain in the Spirit*. This term, however, implies a violence that simply doesn't correspond to the peaceful nature of what I observe happening, so I personally don't like it.

Slain, moreover, connotes death, while most people who experience this phenomenon report that they feel more *alive* than ever interiorly. What people report is quite the opposite of death; the body may seem to die, but that's because, inside, the person's spirit is filled with too much life for the body to contain! The spirit's coming alive seems to me far more important than the body's being slain!

In the Protestant revivals of the nineteenth century, the "Great Awakenings," we find the evangelists using such terms as *falling under the power, fainting* and *being overcome by the Spirit*. These are certainly more positive ways of labeling the phenomenon. More recently (in the past ten years) some theologians have preferred to concentrate on the bodily, external aspect of the experience, separating it from any supernatural explanation. To them the certain thing is that people fall; the uncertain part is the cause. They sincerely question, moreover, whether the falling is brought about by God. So they want to drop *in the Spirit* or *under the power* and call it by a neutral term: the *falling phenomenon*.

These authorities do well to remind us that not everything we see in a healing service is supernatural, and not every supernatural occurrence is caused by God. Certainly I have seen people pushed over, and I have seen people apparently knocked down by evil spirits. "Teacher, I brought you my son, who is possessed by a spirit that has robbed him of speech. Whenever it seizes him, it throws him to the ground" (Mark 9:17–18). I'm also convinced that some of the falling we see is caused by the power of suggestion.

Still, I think we are being overly cautious if we limit ourselves exclusively to the antiseptic term *the falling phenomenon*. It sounds as if we're standing at a great distance from the individuals involved. In addition, the term emphasizes the unimportant part: what happens to the body. As far as I can see, that's a minor matter. The inner component—when it is there—is the important factor.

To ignore the inner experience can be to equate "falling" in a Christian healing service with the totally different, but externally similar, manifestations of voodoo and other magic rites. Cardinal Suenens indeed makes this connection: "Falling was known not only in religions of the past, but it is also found today among different sects, in the

Orient as well as among the primitive tribes of Africa and Latin America."[2]

To compare what happens in Christian ministry to what happens when witch doctors pray is, I believe, to overlook the spiritual reality altogether. I have preached in the Orient, in Africa and in Latin America and I have found that the people themselves are very aware of the difference between what is demonic and what is of God. In our healing services they come in great numbers to be freed of the fearful demonic powers in their lives.

I believe that if the minister of prayer is a committed Christian, with reasonably pure motives, and if the people seeking healing have a basically pure motivation, most of what we see take place will be under the influence of the Holy Spirit—accompanied by the mixture of psychological phenomena that we will always find in our fallen human condition.

In the history of the Catholic Church, a phenomenon that bears some similarities to what we are talking about is called being "rapt in ecstasy"—the term *ecstasy* coming from two Greek words meaning "to stand outside the body." Traditionally some saints during prayer have gone into a trancelike state so intense that they were no longer aware of what was going on around them. Saint Catherine of Siena, for example, got so absorbed in prayer that skeptical members of the papal court at Avignon would stick needles into her to see if she would jump. (She didn't.)

In the summer of 1975 in England, when people began to fall while we were praying for them, the wise and witty Monsignor John O'Connor came up with still another term. He suggested that the reserved British would better accept what was going on if we called it "a touch of dormition."

In the mid-1970s, looking for a term to best describe what we saw happening, I discussed the matter with Father Michael Scanlan (now the president of Steubenville University). We came up with: people being "overcome by the Spirit" in order to "rest in the Spirit." Since then, the term *resting in the Spirit* has come into common usage replacing the more dramatic expressions that highlight the sensational.

There is a wonderful description of resting in the Spirit, using those very words, by Saint Brigitta of Sweden (1303–1373):

> O sweetest God, strange it is what Thou dost to me! For Thou dost put my body to sleep, and my soul Thou awakenest to see and hear and feel the things of the spirit. When it pleaseth Thee, Thou dost send my body to sleep, not with bodily sleep, but with the rest of the spirit, and my soul Thou dost awaken as though from a trance to see and hear and feel with the powers of the spirit.[3]

Who's in Control?

How we react to the sight of people falling down in a healing service, and the words we use to describe what we see, come down often, it seems to me, to a question of control. Leaders who are themselves extremely self-controlled and who plan their church services in minute detail tend to become nervous about anything that departs from a predetermined program. In their writings they usually have a lot to say about "hysteria" and "emotion-alism."

John Wimber tells about how, in one of his powerful encounters with God, he seemed to hear Jesus say, *Give My Church back to Me.* Personally, I believe the symbolic meaning of resting in the Spirit is that God is doing something in our ministry that knocks the props out from under us, literally and figuratively. It is not something that the person who falls is doing by his or her own effort, still less anything initiated by the one who prays. It is God taking charge at a time in history when there is much concentration on human effort—self-improvement courses, salvation by education, the limitless possibilities of our liberated humanity. The New Age movement proclaims that we are gods who can do anything we set our minds to. And here is God knocking people off their feet and saying, in effect, "Oh no, you can't!"

A powerful episode made this clear to me from the very beginning. It happened in 1971 at a retreat for priests and seminarians. This group had put up considerable resis-tance to the then-new charismatic renewal and to the team we had brought from St. Louis. There was so much dissension that we decided to spend an entire session simply praying together. About a hundred priests and seminarians, with three Visitation sisters who were on our retreat team, were crowded into the prayer room. Most were sitting on the floor because there were only a few chairs. When we asked if anyone felt ready to ask for the baptism of the Spirit, one seminarian, Brother Tony, volunteered. We put one of the chairs in the center and Father Joe Lange and I prayed for him. Everyone was waiting to see if anything was really going to happen to him.

There was a long period of silence, with no apparent change in Tony. Then another seminarian asked for prayer, so I asked Tony if he would move so we could use the chair again. To our surprise he said, "I can't move." Rather than call attention to this strange occurrence, we simply commandeered a second chair. All during the following prayers Tony remained sitting where he was, motionless. After about an hour, he asked a friend to adjust his glasses, since they were slipping down over his nose. Yet he looked all right and was able to talk. So we did nothing, trying not to call attention to Tony's embarrassing plight in front of this critical group.

When the meeting broke up at last, more than two hours later, Tony remained behind, immobile. Our team gathered quickly around him. Finally he said, "I seem to keep hearing, 'Without Me you can do nothing.' During my whole life I have always tried to control everything. Now I'm going to have to turn my life over to God." Once he said that he began to move, and five minutes later he was able to stand up and leave the room. At the time it seemed like a rather dramatic acted-out word from God. Only later did I connect it in my mind with what I had witnessed at the Kathryn Kuhlman service.

The seminarian was sitting in a chair, not standing. We were not expecting anyone to rest in the Spirit; we hardly knew what it was in those days. It certainly was not hypnotically induced.

I know that fine theologians, devout Christians, question whether the falling phenomenon isn't mostly a psychologically induced behavior. My own experience leads me to believe that most of what we see (but not all) is directed by the Holy Spirit: that it is a striking demonstration of what happens when human finiteness makes contact with God. The person who rests surrenders control. While we may say that we desire to surrender our lives to God, many of us don't really want to. I know that some evangelists make a show out of people being slain in the Spirit and lay too much emphasis on miraculous signs (see 1 Corinthians 1:22).

Nevertheless, I believe that the sight of people overcome by the Spirit is not meant to lead to pride, but is on the contrary a demonstration of human weakness intended to produce humility.

> But God chose the foolish things of the world to shame the wise; God chose the weak things of the world to shame the strong. . . . so that no one may boast before him.   1 Corinthians 1:27–29

2
What Happens When People Fall?

What is resting in the Spirit? There are many explanations, ranging all the way from mass hysteria and auto-hypnosis to a gifting of the Spirit. At times it can be any of these, but I really believe that the spiritual attitude of the person doing the praying and of the person being prayed for preclude the less desirable manifestations. At our healing services, some people may talk themselves into falling, but even then no great harm is done. The vast majority seem to experience a beneficial spiritual effect.

At a four-day conference on inner healing here in Jacksonville in 1988, we asked the group of 250 how many had experienced a *"significant* inner healing in some area of their lives." About ninety percent raised their hands, which is an extraordinary response. While some were healed through prayer in the small groups, many, if not most, reported that they'd been healed while resting in the Spirit following a brief individual prayer during our large healing service.

Someday, perhaps, a biologist or psychologist will adequately describe the state of a person resting in the Spirit.

Certainly it varies, both as to the physical reactions and the spiritual content. Until then, I would like to share what we have seen and heard firsthand from the many people we have prayed with (and from the reading we have done).

Physical Reactions

One thing I have noticed is that a person resting in the Spirit usually shows normal physical signs; his or her pulse and respiration remain normal. Dr. David Lewis in his report on the John Wimber conference in Harrogate, England, found that many of the people there experienced changes in their breathing. But we see very little of this at our meetings. I remember hearing at the 1975 international conference of Roman Catholic charismatics in Rome, while all 10,000 of us were gathered in St. Peter's, that someone had unexpectedly been overcome by the Spirit. The on-lookers wanted to call an ambulance, but the Swiss guard who came over to investigate said not to bother; he could tell by the person's vital signs that he was not sick or distressed but was having a spiritual experience.

In *some* people who are resting you will see fluttering eyelids, the rapid eye movement (REM) that we all have when we dream during sleep. Since many people while resting experience visions, I have always wondered if those fluttering eyelids are not a sign that God is gifting that person with an inner vision.

Occasionally a person we pray for experiences an altered state of consciousness while remaining standing. When we return to that same spot, after going down the line to pray for various needs, we find the person still standing there, eyes closed. Something is clearly going on within that individual. This "standing phenomenon" indicates that the primary component of this experience is not exterior—the position of the body—but interior. After a time the person "comes to," as it were, and walks away, often with the sense of having been in God's presence in a special way.

I remember one lady at a conference in Washington, D.C., who remained upright while people to the right and left of her had fallen to the floor. An erect and dignified Englishwoman, she exhibited only one outward sign of experiencing anything out of the ordinary: Her head lolled to one side, then rolled repeatedly in circles!

Telling friends about it later, she recalled that the motion had been entirely involuntary. And custom-made for her need: "All the while, I heard God saying to me, 'Cecily, you must lose your stiffnecked attitude!' "

God had ministered to Cecily with a minimum of external effect.

Some people, on the other hand, have a dramatic physical reaction, while the inner component seems negligible. This has been my own pattern; I personally have fallen about fifteen times, but have never had a significant healing or spiritual experience (much as I would like to).

Others fall and after a time try to get up but are unable to move. Just last week at a healing service a woman rested after I prayed for her. After about five minutes she decided she had better get up. She tried, but it was too soon; she fell back and hurt her head. Later she came through the line a second time asking for a prayer to heal her head. (Yes, it was healed.) For her, apparently, the *inner* experience had come to a close while the *physical* part was still in effect.

So we get all these variants: Some people experience only the inner component, with a slight physical accompaniment (e.g., those who remain standing), while others experience just the falling, with nothing much happening in the interior order. In short, two phenomena seem to be involved: a manifestation of *God's power*, leading to the body's falling, and/or a *healing* component, occurring within the individual's spirit.

Conscious, But Not Able to Move

Although *fainting* and *swooning* were words often used in the last century to describe the falling phenomenon, it is not really that. By and large people do not become unconscious; on the contrary, they report a higher degree of consciousness than ever—so much so that it drains energy away from the body. The person usually remains aware of what is going on around him, but it is a detached awareness.

> I was conscious and could vaguely hear—when I chose to listen—but could not see or speak. When I heard the lady asking everybody to leave I tried to get up, but when I lifted up, my head was pulled back to the ground. There seemed to be a great weight on top of me which I was not conscious of until I tried to get up. When I tried to say, "I'm not able to leave," I discovered I could say no words except "Praise God," "Jesus" or pray in tongues. I was conscious of light shocks and twitches inside my head and body and a feeling of peace similar to an anesthetic. I heard

someone say, "We are carrying you to another room"; I was conscious of being lifted but could do nothing to help. Eventually I sat up after being sort of "out of the body" for 45 minutes. I just had time to get to the terminal five minutes before the bus left for the plane I was to catch.

Or again, as Teresa of Avila (1515–1582) describes her condition when "rapt in ecstasy":

> The subject rarely loses consciousness; I have sometimes lost it altogether, but only seldom and for but a short time. As a rule the consciousness is disturbed; and though incapable of action with respect to outward things, the subject can still hear and understand, but only dimly, as though from a long way off. . . .[1]

The *position* of the body is not as important as its temporary loss of motion. As St. Teresa writes:

> The position, then, is that, however hard I try, my body, for considerable periods, has not the strength to make it capable of movement: all its strength has been taken away by the soul. . . .
>
> For, while the rapture lasts, the body often remains dead and unable of itself to do anything; it continues all the time as it was when the rapture came upon it—in a sitting position, for example, or with the hands open or shut.

Similarly, a woman at Wimber's Harrogate conference, while mentally and spiritually awake, was physically immobile:

My mother and sister next to me thought I'd fallen asleep but I could remember all John [Wimber] had said but couldn't move physically. The strange thing was it didn't bother me—I felt at peace with the situation.

At the coffee break they tried to wake me up and were worried when they couldn't. . . . They actually called for an ambulance and I was taken to the . . . general hospital. . . . On the way I consciously heard all my mother and her friend were saying to me but I was unable to respond. . . . All I can say is, it seemed looking back that the Lord had separated part of me from my body—a lot of inner healing was taking place there.[2]

In this account we find three pertinent observations:

1) The woman was sitting, not standing (though if she had been standing she probably would have fallen);

2) John Wimber was at some distance and was not praying for her individually;

3) Her inability to move her body helped what was happening in her spirit.

Peace and Gentleness

In our healing services the people who rest are ordinarily peaceful and quiet. Our services are deliberately unemotional; we ask for quiet and usually have a gentle accompaniment of singing or music. We usually pray quietly in tongues, but occasionally we pray in English if there seems to be an advantage to that.

While we are praying, some people seem to be filled to the brim, as it were, with God's love and when they are full they fall back gently and rest—most of them quietly. (We will talk about the exceptions later.) Some get up quickly, while others may rest for minutes, or even hours.

When people fall, they often report having experienced a feeling of weightlessness, as in the following excerpts from letters sent to me:

> As you placed your hands very lightly on my forehead, a feeling of weightlessness came over me as I went down. There was this feeling of peace. Although I was semi-conscious, it was as if I were in another world which was very peaceful.

> Then I got this feeling like I was falling and I could feel Father's hands grasping my head, as if to keep me from falling. Then I just went down like a feather, so softly. I felt weightless, but I was always conscious; I just had no control over my body. I wanted to get up, but I couldn't move so I just stayed there, realizing for the first time in my life that Jesus loved me and forgave me my sins.

I remember once, with a group of priests in Australia, that one priest was determined not to fall when I prayed with him. Then he experienced a floating sensation and felt a strong impression that he was going to go up! Quickly he decided that he would be much less conspicuous if he went down—which he promptly did. Curiously, while some people feel *weightless*, as if they are floating, others feel the opposite—a kind of *heaviness* that keeps them on the ground.

Choice

As such accounts suggest, the individual often has a choice in the reaction he experiences. He can elect to surrender and fall back, or else he can plant his feet firmly and remain standing.

Surrender can feel a little like death. Dr. John White records what happened to one English clergyman, John Mumford, at a conference where John Wimber—from a distance, without laying hands on the man—simply invited the Holy Spirit to come. In his diary John Mumford shares what happened:

> I can only describe the whole thing as a process of dying. I felt afterward like Sir Walter Raleigh's cloak after Queen Elizabeth had walked over it; or I felt like I'd been rolled over by a steam roller! God had sat on me.
>
> The whole thing must have lasted one and a half hours and by the end I felt blitzed. I lay on my back for what seemed like a long time, unable to move, with my arms outstretched on the floor in a cruciform shape—if it's not blasphemy, the significance was not lost on me.
>
> . . . That night in bed and again next morning, I felt the Spirit on me—the energy, the trembling, feeling as if my body was quaking and shaking inside, tho' it wasn't outwardly. All I can say by way of explanation at this point is that it was a visitation by the Holy Spirit—bypassing the mind maybe for no

other purpose than to establish and deepen my relationship with the Lord.[3]

Dr. White, as a psychiatrist, goes on to say that the Rev. John Mumford was not a hysterical person. Mumford believed, moreover, that he could initially have resisted and blocked what was happening to him but that he could not have produced these symptoms himself.

I have seen people, on the other hand, who did try to resist this power but, like Saul on the road to Damascus, were felled to the ground.

Whether or not the person is able to resist this impulse, it does seem that "falling under the power" is precisely that: the person is not initiating the action of his own volition but is somehow "acted upon."

> I felt the back of my calf shaking in a way one can't do oneself. . . . I felt it coming up my back and shaking everywhere, but particularly noticed it in places where I wouldn't normally shake—muscular spasms which I've not had before or since.

> Envelope of "energy"?—difficult to describe. Cone of power/energy descended on me.

> Force field coming over me like rain running down from head to toe. It was like something out of Star Wars.[4]

Dr. White writes about Sandy who

> heard group members praying in tongues, felt what she describes as a bolt of energy going through her

and fell. As she lay there she was aware continuously of energy passing through her body, but of little else. She knew that the meeting was going on . . . but she felt totally detached.

After what seemed to her like ten or fifteen minutes (actually three and a half hours), she got up. . . . As her mind recovered its sharp contact with time and space, she became aware of an even greater restoration of her sense of self-worth—as a child of God. No longer was it dependent on her job or her role in life. This recovery of self-worth has been an enduring one.[5]

Interestingly, with the passage of time we notice that the bodily manifestations associated with spiritual phenomena grow less pronounced. In Catholic spiritual tradition it has long been observed that the body is at first overwhelmed by God's presence but, in time, grows used to it, so that mature Christians will gradually show fewer of these external reactions. Dr. White comes to the same conclusion:

What initially may have been impossible to control progressively becomes easier to control. Paul assures us, for instance, that speaking in a tongue and uttering prophecies (the exercise of Spirit-imparted gifts) are under the voluntary control of individual Christians. The Spirit may inspire, but the Christian chooses when to utter. "The spirits of prophets are subject to the control of prophets" (1 Cor. 14:32).

Repeated manifestations are also under the voluntary control of the individual or become so within a relatively short time. This does not necessarily mean that they can "turn it on" whenever they choose, but that when the Holy Spirit is powerfully present they can choose to suppress or allow the manifestation to take place.

Causation

People falling over after prayer can have three possible causes:

1) The *supernatural* power of *God;*

2) A *natural* psychological power (e.g., suggestion) invested in some charismatic figure in whom people believe;

3) The *preternatural* power of the *demonic* realm.

I believe that I have seen all these powers at work from time to time. The difficulty is that you cannot discern the cause simply by looking on and watching people fall. The purely physical aspect, the falling, may happen when Christians pray, but also when shamans and witch doctors pray. Externally the result is similar—though the cause (and also the spiritual effect, when present) are totally different. We cannot *see* the power of God, nor the power of suggestion, nor the demonic realm (unless God endows us with the gift of discerning spirits).

This same question of causation is true of all spiritual gifts. Healing, for instance, can be brought about

1) By God's power—a *supernatural* gift of healing;

2) By the body's own *natural* recuperative power;

3) Through the influence of the *mind over the body* (the "placebo effect");

4) By *demonic* forces (witchcraft).

We effectively rule out healing by demonic forces by making sure that both the minister of prayer and the sick person have turned to Jesus Christ as the source of healing. It is the same with falling under the power. By exalting Jesus we try to make our broken humanity as pure a channel for the Holy Spirit as we can.

In Scripture, too, we find examples of similar external phenomena, some caused by the power of God, and others by demons. The apostle John, for instance, writes, "When I saw him, I fell at his feet as though dead" (Revelation 1:17). We also read, on the other hand, about a father bringing his son to Jesus for a cure: "When the spirit saw Jesus, it immediately threw the boy into a convulsion. He fell to the ground and rolled around, foaming at the mouth" (Mark 9:20).

Both of these accounts involve falling to the ground, but no one doubts that John's reaction was due to a visitation from God, while the boy was thrown down by an evil spirit. Part of the discernment here is through the effect: The boy writhes and suffers in a way that makes onlookers infer that an evil spirit is at work.

The Effects

Similarly, we can judge what kind of power is at work during our services by observing the effects on the people who rest. "By their fruits you shall know them" is the best way—the only way, really—of judging whether the experience is of God. What we find is that an extraordinary number of people have encountered Jesus Christ in a life-transforming way upon falling down. For some it leads to repentance, for others to a greater love for God; others are healed, especially in their inner beings; still others are delivered of evil spirits. Not everyone experiences something significant in the spiritual realm, but even those who don't are made aware of the power of God as they fall.

In short, the fact that people fall says very little about the phenomenon. It says nothing about its real meaning— about what causes the person to fall or about the effects of the experience. I believe, though, that

1) We can avoid most of the questionable causes of people falling if we pray with a pure motivation.

2) For some people who fall there may be a strong psychological component (the power of suggestion); however, we have so far not been able to discover any noteworthy negative consequences following these auto-induced experiences.

3) Some people will fall simply because of God's power (as often seemed to happen in Kathryn Kuhlman's ministry) while nothing particular happens in the spiritual order. (In other words, there is a strong physical effect, but little spiritual effect.)

4) Many people will not only fall but will experience a marked spiritual transformation and/or healing.

As one minister wrote to John Wimber after a conference in Sheffield, England:

> Please, could you please tell me what exactly you proclaimed in your blessing on the Thursday night in Sheffield!
>
> I heard about the first three sentences and then POW!! It was incredible. God fell on me, I was utterly broken, my whole life before him on the line. I thought he was going to kill me. . . . It was awesome and painful, as what felt like high-voltage electricity burned through me.
>
> Friends around me described it like I was being stretched. There appeared to be a force around me. And this lasted about fifteen minutes, and then I thought I had died because my body seemed filled, transparent with light.[6]

Later this minister wrote:

> Sheffield marked a turning point in my life. In terms of subsequent growth and usefulness to the Lord it has been one of the most significant experiences since conversion. . . .
>
> In my ministry I have found authority and a greater expectancy of God to work than ever before.

3
Why Is It Helpful to Rest in the Spirit?

When people are overcome by the Spirit, the all-important inner component varies from a person's just receiving a nice little rest all the way to having a life-transforming encounter with the living God. Let me share with you from among the experiences that hundreds of people have shared with me.

The first thing that strikes me is that the overwhelming majority of people who have fallen under the power report that it was a happy experience. I am always surprised to notice that even those who express the most caution about the falling phenomenon, when they get down to listing what people say who have actually fallen, describe almost altogether positive experiences. Cardinal Suenens, for example, in *Resting in the Spirit*, lists as fruits cited by his correspondents:

- The alleviation of psychic disturbances;

- Almost total healing of profound psychic problems;

- The healing of inner wounds and resentments;

- The healing of damaged relationships (marriage, etc.);

- Feelings of peace;

- New possibilities of forgiving or repenting;

- A love of prayer and Scripture; a depth of encounter with Jesus;

- Some physical healings (rare).[1]

Here is an overview of the exciting positive results we ourselves have observed when people rest in the Spirit.

A Demonstration of God's Power

The first (and most common) result of falling under the power is that it impresses people—onlookers as well as those who experience it—as an extraordinary demonstration of God's omnipotence. This is the way I see it used in most evangelistic healing services. People fall over and the assemblage, as it were, gasps. Here it truly is the falling phenomenon. Concentration is on the outer manifestation and what apparently causes it: God's power. It is helpful because it impresses the whole congregation with the overwhelming presence of God. People fall into the arms of catchers who get them back up almost immediately on their feet. Whole rows are sometimes swept down as the minister of healing walks by. As young people today say, "It's awesome!"

Often the minister (Kathryn Kuhlman did this, as does Benny Hinn today) prays individually for the sick person only *after* the person testifies to his healing; then that person usually falls to the floor.

What happens on the inside of the person when he falls seems to be generally neglected in such meetings; understanding of falling is mostly limited to this vivid experience of God's power. In today's rationalistic world, experiencing (or seeing) God's power at work is a very worthwhile evangelistic purpose. (Admittedly it caters to those who gravitate toward the spectacular, and the evangelist can be tempted to glory in his "pipeline to God.") The interior benefit to the person falling can be limited in such a meeting to simply *feeling*: "Wow! What hit me? I've never experienced the power of God like that!"

Even so, I believe this kind of dramatic experience can be a real benefit to most people—including most ministers and priests—in our overly scientific, materialistic society.

An Intimate Experience of God's Presence

A significant number of people have spoken or written to me about the life-transforming visions they experienced while resting. Although the resting phenomenon is certainly not necessary for a person to experience Jesus' presence, it does seem helpful. With the body out of the way, so to speak, the person can concentrate more fully on what is happening within. (In the same way we often hear Him most clearly during sleep.) Distractions grow less and we are better able to listen.

In fact, one complaint that we often receive from people resting in the Spirit is that the music was too loud or that someone leaned down and prayed loudly over them.

As a result they found it hard to concentrate on what the Lord was showing them.

In this resting state, then, we find that God is free to meet people at the very heart of their being. As one teacher expressed it:

> How I wish I could find words to express my profound gratitude for the deep joy and abiding peace that have invaded my being during these past few weeks as I continue to grow in the Spirit. One of the most beautiful gifts that has come to me is to know that Jesus is Lord and Savior and that He really cares. I have always known this intellectually, and we even "teach" it to our students. But to know this in truth and, in fact, to feel it deep inside the marrow of my bones, has made all the difference in the world. . . .
>
> To be able to come to a deeper sense of awareness and to know for sure that Jesus is for real . . . that He loves me beyond my wildest dreams and imagination. This is a miracle and more; it is life, His life, His love.
>
> I want to shout out to the whole world, "Come, see and taste and know that the Lord is God, and good, and all loving and kind."

These words do not come from a high school girl but a forty-year-old woman with many years of teaching experience.

Sometimes when we pray for people, the specific healing requested does not take place, yet there is a real gift of God's presence—such as is described in the following letter:

On June 11, 1975, when you so kindly offered personal ministry, you laid hands on me and prayed for the healing of arthritis, a hiatal hernia and sinusitis. The awareness of the presence of Jesus and the joy were so intense that I was overpowered in the Spirit. That awareness stays with me, although I have not received the healing physically. The really important thing is that I know Jesus better each day.

Many times this encounter leads to a deepened commitment. During the International Charismatic Conference in Rome in May 1975, for instance, I prayed for the healing of a woman who had been in an auto accident more than ten years before, and who was still suffering its effects throughout her body. After she prayed for ten minutes, the pain and other side effects left her and she was rejoicing. (She was not overcome in the Spirit.) Later in the day, however, I saw her again and she looked downcast. When I asked her what was wrong, she said that all the pain was back, worse than ever. So I began to pray again and asked the Lord if He wished to deal with this problem through the power of the Spirit. This time she fell and rested for about five minutes; then she stood up again, radiant. She had seen a dazzling light and said that she heard the Lord tell her, "Surrender yourself to Me and I will heal you." She did surrender, and this time the healing was permanent.

Some theologians warn about the dangers of people seeking the experience rather than seeking God. Assuredly this is a real possibility. But for the most part I think people are seeking God *in* the experience, the experience *of God*; they are helped to love God by this experience. It really helps most people if, at some point in their lives, they come to know God in an intimate way. It helps us later during our dry desert periods to remember those times when we sensed acutely the nearness of God. Indeed, I believe it is God's ordinary approach to give people some kind of religious experience as they begin their spiritual journey: Moses saw the burning bush and heard God's voice; Paul was thrown to the ground and a light from heaven flashed around him.

Other theologians question whether such experiences have any lasting effect on a person's life. Sometimes not. But inconsistency should be no surprise in our human affairs; does everyone who hears an inspired sermon, for that matter, lead a transformed life from that moment on? Yet I do find an extraordinary number of people whose lives seem permanently affected by the experience of resting in the Spirit. For example:

> I experienced a deep peace and it seemed as if I were floating. I was totally overcome by the Spirit. I have never in my life experienced Jesus so beautifully. Ever since, my relationship with Jesus has really grown and I have a new awareness of Him, whether at school, home or whatever. And I know this isn't meant to be an experience and then it's over. I know it is meant that I grow more aware of His presence in my life.

Sometimes this presence is experienced in the form of angels. Dr. David Lewis quotes a letter from a 39-year-old man who attended John Wimber's Harrogate conference:

> One time when I was in the center of the hall, when I went down I was aware of a whole lot of

angelic activity in the room—it was very soothing and very beautiful. As if a lot of angels—I couldn't actually see their form but I could see the effect, like wind stirring up leaves. Like a whirlwind of angelic activity going up to the ceiling and then coming down to people, and I could hear the faint hum of angelic harmony as they went, in praise—I felt that's what it was. Like leaves spiraling up and down in the wind. . . .[2]

An Impetus to Conversion or Repentance

Many times, too, people report a fundamental change of will. Anglican Bishop David Pytches gives a remarkable example of conversion while resting in the Spirit:

> About six months ago a lady came forward following evening worship in the church and knelt at the rails. She asked for prayer concerning a thyroid condition. My wife encouraged her to relax and invoked the Holy Spirit to come and minister to her. A few seconds later she was falling backwards. Her husband came forward believing she had fainted and wanted to put her head between her knees to revive her, but was deterred when trying to touch her head and he felt "currents" of power coming from her. She remained on the floor for some fifteen minutes or so, after which she got to her feet, thanked those who had prayed for her and departed. The following day she phoned up, identifying herself as the one prayed for who had keeled over. She said, "Hullo, my name is . . . I am a Jewess, but I want to be baptized. I have become a believer in Jesus." She was recently

confirmed by the Bishop of St. Alban's. Glory be to God![3]

Dr. Lewis notes that many people experience a sense of being cleansed:

> . . . I knew I was OK and supposed to be on the floor and the Lord was doing something. Afterwards, I felt turned inside-out and scrubbed so clean it was unbelievable.[4]

This cleansing often involves repentance, as in this account by a man who was led to acknowledge his adultery:

> D. began to pray for me [for healing] but nothing happened. He asked if . . . anything needed to be put right. There was—about immorality a long time ago. I needed to put it right.
>
> I was in a quandary because I didn't really want to put it right and I didn't want to be "slain in the Spirit." . . . Then my whole body began to twitch. He prayed harder. "Lord, let him see your love." I shook quite uncontrollably against the seats around me and there was nothing I could do to stop it.
>
> In the middle of all this . . . a ray of light came into my presence—like I'm there in this seat shaking and I know where I am, I've got my eyes shut, but it seemed as if in the darkness of my eyes shut, a beam of light came in and a burden lifted off me.
>
> The peace and overwhelming security that came with that was quite remarkable. I didn't want to let it go, but I came back into reality when he ended his prayer. It seemed as if I was free and hadn't been free

for a long time. After that I was able to join in worship—I hadn't been fully able to for three days. I also realized I'd been hardened in my attitude and now wasn't so.

When I got home I had to put it right with my wife and confess to her. On Monday at work I was looking out the window at the landscape garden: it was as if the beauty of the Lord came into that garden and I began to cry—it's not like me, I'm not a person who cries—so I knew that what had happened was a real experience.[5]

An Environment for Healing

Of all the extraordinary things that happen while people are resting, healing seems to be the most common.

I have seen so many powerful healings take place when a person is overcome in the Spirit that I have come to recognize it as a wonderful aid to the healing ministry—if and when God chooses to grant it as His free gift. It is as if the Lord Himself moves in and works far more powerfully than we could ever hope or imagine. It is almost always peaceful, except in those cases where the healing hand of God touches deep hurts and the person starts to weep, or when the power of God comes up against demonic opposition.

I have seen every kind of healing take place while people were resting in the Spirit, all the way from the healing of bones to the deepest spiritual transformation.

I have found the overpowering of the Spirit an especially important help to facilitate healing when there is no time to really talk and pray as one would like to, such as when ministering to very large crowds. Often, especially at healing services in which there are long lines, when I don't know what's wrong and don't have time to ask, the Lord will simply deal with the problem Himself.

Father Benedict Haren, for instance, who had suffered from mental depression for years, asked if I would pray with him. Since there were many people waiting for prayer, I prayed for him just briefly in tongues. Soon he was overcome in the Spirit and rested for some two hours. During that time, the Lord came and took him through his entire life, stage by stage, explaining the meaning of his painful experiences, and then healing them. Some things the priest had thought were important turned out to be relatively unimportant. On the other hand, Jesus showed him nearly forgotten incidents that had left him with deep wounds. One teaching the Lord gave him has especially remained with me: "Do you realize that the people you forgive, I will forgive, too? You can truly loose your enemies."

As he later wrote:

> In 1975 when Francis MacNutt prayed over me in a healing service I "rested in the Spirit" for two hours and twenty minutes. During that time I not only realized that I had not forgiven certain people, a fact I was unaware of before, but I also learned more about the nature and demands of Christian forgiveness while lying on the ground there than I had ever understood from talks or books. The Holy Spirit gave me a much deeper insight on this subject, which I regard as one of the major spiritual blessings of my life.[6]

Fr. Haren was healed through a one-minute prayer (on my part) that turned out better than if I had spent hours counseling and praying with him. I should emphasize here, though, that this kind of thing happens only occasionally; usually such deep inner healing takes time. Even when a person is overcome by the Spirit, it doesn't necessarily mean that the healing is complete. Later we may need to talk and pray over an extended time, just as we would ordinarily.

I have also found resting in the Spirit to be helpful when evil spirits are present. It makes our task much easier when the power of God is so strong that anything evil has a hard time surviving in its presence. Demonic forces are driven off by the excess of God's goodness and don't have to be cast out directly. Or, if direct confrontation and casting out are needed, the evil spirits surrender more easily.

This is also true of healing. This special power seems to make healing easier; more seems to take place and it happens more quickly. It's as if the Lord Himself takes over and gives the wounded the counseling and restoration they need:

> I asked for the spirit of anxiety to be taken away from me and the infilling of His peace. As you prayed over me a great power forced me back. I was trying to stay on my feet; as the force became less I could see a bright light and I was as if caught up in it. I've never seen anything so bright. I remember singing joyfully as I witnessed this brightness.
>
> The next morning I awoke in a spirit of peace I have never known, and I could smell the scent of roses. . . . I was in that state of peace for quite a few days.

We need also to mention what should perhaps be obvious:

Not everyone is healed. At times when I have prayed for people to be healed and they have been overcome in the Spirit, no healing has followed. They may have had an experience of peace, or they may even have felt some kind of deep spiritual union with God. But that doesn't necessarily mean they have been physically or emotionally healed.

It probably shouldn't be necessary to say this, after everything else I have written about people not being healed. But so many people are disappointed when their expectations don't come true immediately that it's important to help them to accept the inward blessing they do receive and not lose it because of a false guilt about not receiving something else.

This said, however, resting in the Spirit seems to be a state in which a person is more likely to receive healing. At times it almost seems like the anesthetic for an operation in which a person is put to rest so that God can perform necessary surgery. At times the surgery is brief; at other times it may be a six-hour undertaking.

I should also add that I do not believe resting in the Spirit is necessary or *causes* healing. The resting is just a helpful, relaxed condition to be in for healing to take place. Certainly most healing that comes about through prayer is not accompanied by resting. Yet I also believe that being overcome in the Spirit is a sign of the presence and power of the Spirit. That power of the Holy Spirit is what causes healing, so resting is a hopeful sign that healing is taking place.

Healing of Body and Spirit

Physical Healing

Although inner healing is reported more frequently when people rest in the Spirit, perhaps five times as often, still a significant number of people receive bodily healing while they are resting.

Here is one woman's report:

> After the experience, all pain, muscle spasms, tensions and pressures in my head, neck, arm, shoulder, upper and lower back and right leg were completely gone. The following five days, totally free of any kind of discomfort, was the longest period of such freedom from pain, etc., since the car accident eleven years ago. Since the end of those five days, varying degrees of muscle spasms, tension and pressures that result in the buildup of pain have returned, but the pain has greatly lessened as have all the other symptoms. My husband and I pray for the continued fullness of His healing power every day. Sometimes after praying, the pain will go again completely. My doctor, an orthopedic surgeon who has been treating me every other week for a year and a half, confirmed last week a "100-percent improvement" in the condition of all areas. For the first time since coming to him because of acute chronic muscle spasm (with three vertebrae, seven discs, both left and right sacroiliac pulled out, causing leg and arm nerve damage), this last visit everything was in place! The first and second layers of muscle were relaxed to the point that for the first time he could reach and work with that most severely injured third layer of muscles in my neck

and shoulder! And a blocked, damaged nerve that had resisted any treatment was healed, freeing the use of my right thumb.

The doctor spoke about my experience as having in some way been the source of accelerated healing, and that the days that followed free of all pain were a time of the body being taught how to be free of spasms, etc. He believes now the healing will progress more rapidly to a completion than it probably ever could have before.

Bishop David Pytches recounts the following story:

Some two years ago a boy came forward for prayer in St. Andrew's. He had a history of epilepsy, was small, hyperactive and behind in his schoolwork due to this affliction. The Holy Spirit was invoked to come upon him, and a few seconds later he fell to the floor. He looked so white and still that at least one person thought he had died and was only comforted by reflecting that when Jesus ministered to an epileptic he fell and appeared "like a corpse" (Mark 9:26). After a while the boy seemed to revive and his parents took him home and put him to bed. He slept for fourteen hours; in fact, he slept so much the following week that he could not go to school. Since that day he has never had a single "fit." He has grown several inches. By the time this is in print he will have taken several O-levels at school. His doctor has just seen him and says there is no reason why he should not drive a motorbike. This was the Lord's doing and marvellous in our eyes![7]

One unusual instance I remember: I was going into a meeting hall to give a talk when a woman stopped me and asked me to pray to straighten out her hammer toes. Ordinarily I would have knelt down with my hands on her feet but since I was expected at that moment on the platform, I merely put my hands on her head and prayed briefly. I was not really expecting her to fall, but she did as the power of God coursed down to her feet. And her hammer toes straightened out!

Inner Healing

Inner healing is by far the most frequent benefit reported after resting in the Spirit. By inner healing I simply mean God's healing of our spirits and damaged emotions, in distinction to His healing our bodily ailments. In inner healing God takes the poison out of all of those spiritual and emotional wounds, often inflicted in childhood, that prevent us from being free to think, feel and act in the way we know deep-down we should. Inner healing is Jesus freeing us from the miserable situation described by Paul:

> I do not understand what I do. For what I want to do I do not do, but what I hate I do. . . . For I have the desire to do what is good, but I cannot carry it out. For what I do is not the good I want to do; no, the evil I do not want to do—this I keep on doing.
> Romans 7:15, 18–19

In our services many people report an integration of this deeply divided self. Usually the people resting are fully conscious but are simply not as aware of the outside world as usual. This makes it easier for them to concentrate on whatever the Lord might be revealing to them at the time. Some people see visions; others receive a deep insight into the roots of their problems. At times Jesus will heal a problem without the person's precise knowledge of what it is. The person can say only, "Something left me. I have no idea what it was, but now I feel different. More important, I now act differently."

Most often, however, we find Jesus doing two things:

1) *Surfacing the problem,* so that the person can see it: bringing it out of darkness into light;

2) *Healing it,* once it has been brought into the light.

One of those important elements that the Lord surfaces is hidden sin. At the Rome conference I mentioned earlier, for instance, one friend asked me to pray for her. We were in the midst of a large, noisy crowd, meeting above the Catacombs, and I didn't expect her to fall, but she did. When she got up a few minutes later, all she could say was, "Jesus told me to repent."

We have received many beautiful letters describing the amazing things Jesus does while people are resting. Here's an excerpt from one of them:

> When I came to ask you for healing, I knew that I needed inner healing. . . . I was so heavily burdened and weighed down with so much pain that I couldn't see straight or think clearly. All I knew was that I was hurting and bleeding inside.
>
> I remember how much junk and chaos was inside me; I was weighed down by my sins and ready to blow my mind away, even questioning my own sanity. The hypocrisy of my life was getting to me—smiling on the outside, pretending that everything was O.K.—while deep inside I was hurting.

And now to feel so light and free—freer than the birds singing with crazy versatility just outside my window, more joyful than the song they are singing, happy to be alive, sooo happy, no longer having to pretend, just free to be me, free to move around, and most of all, free to love everyone, especially those I live with. What an exhilarating experience of being once more with Jesus. And now I know what it means to be singled out just for Jesus. What a joy to be all His!

To me the beautiful thing is to see how tenderly Jesus ministers to each person with an individual healing so creative that I would never have been able to make it up, if I were having to invent a prayer for each and every person. The following is taken (with permission) from the diary of a severely depressed woman who spent a week with us, so that we might pray with her each day:

Judith could not be present, but Francis prayed for me to be released from the spirit of rejection. Then I rested in the Spirit. I sensed God the Father, my Abba, putting His arm around me and showing me when I was a small child. He could not get me to love that little child. Finally I did manage to ask the child if she would forgive me for not loving her all these years.

Then Francis prayed a second time. This time I saw the Lord take me and the child to an ice cream parlor. The parlor had three seats in it: one for Jesus, one for me and one for the child (who, of course, was also me at a younger age). Jesus put His arms around the two of us, while we ate a delicious chocolate sundae. I looked at the little girl, who was simply delighting in her ice cream; her face and little hands were covered with chocolate ice cream. She looked so funny that I started to laugh. And I began to feel a genuine love for her. Jesus was watching the two of us all this time. At last He looked at me and said, "From now on the two of you are going to get along just fine together!"

Since this time, my attitude toward myself has changed as much as night and day. The Lord has taught me to minister to myself in a very loving way; as I do so, I am beginning to have a genuine love for other people. This healing has brought me an awe and wonder of being human. God has placed a very special person in my life to reinforce this truth. And what a joy it is to love another person from the heart. . . . I continue to grow in peace about myself, as well as grow in love of others, with a new freedom that I never knew before. I find my memory clearing and the great emotional overload gradually going away. I am placing a beautiful trust in God also; this trust has led to a new type of free-flowing prayer life within myself.

Through your compassion, God has rolled the stones away from the tomb that had for so many years held me captive!

Following is another tender story of inner healing, this time in the relationship between a three-year-old boy and his mother (I have changed the names):

Francis, you may remember praying for a child and his mother at the same time last night. That mother was me and that child was Joseph. Anyway, it never occurred to me to bring my children to the healing service; I thought it would scare them or that they might be disruptive. But as soon as I saw children being prayed for, I had to go and get Joseph, so I ran up the rainy mountainside to the cabin where my husband was preparing him for bed.

I fetched him and he never cried, wiggled or whimpered. He was so loving, so accepting, so trusting. You prayed for us and we both rested *together* in the Spirit. That has to be from God! What mother in her right mind would fall backwards with a forty-two-pound baby in her arms! He was so precious; he stirred before I did and said, "Mommy, what are you sleeping on the floor for?"

Joseph was my third child. He is only thirteen months younger than his brother Harry. I became pregnant while nursing and nurturing Harry so I found it very difficult to accept that another life inside me also needed nurturing. I was ambivalent about the pregnancy and—yes—a little resentful, only because of the time element involved. I was very ill the entire nine months, and yet I had my other two children to love and provide for.

I did grow to love and accept him as he grew within my womb, and I realized what a wonderful blessing he was when he was born.

But that womb time is what the Lord chose to heal last night. He ministered to us both so that I know, beyond the shadow of a doubt, that Joseph won't have to deal with feelings of rejection at age thirty, since God healed him at age three! He truly reconciled us last night. I rocked him for hours and told him all the things you would like to tell your unborn baby. It was truly a *holy* time, led by the Lord!

Deliverance from Evil Spirits

Most extraordinary of all is when we find evil spirits departing as someone is overcome in the Spirit. As I said earlier, resting in the Spirit is ordinarily quiet and peaceful, but occasionally we see an eruption of demonic resistance. To people unfamiliar with these outbursts, the crying out and/or convulsions can be upsetting and frightening.

The scenes depicted in Jesus' ministry—for example, Mark 1:26: "The evil spirit shook the man violently and came out of him with a shriek"—are unfamiliar to most Christians in our culture today. If Jesus prayed with these dramatic results in one of our mainline churches, He might well be asked to leave! Third World cultures seem far more understanding about what goes on in deliverance than we are. At any rate, in our services—comfortable or not—we have to deal with a certain amount of demonic manifestation.

When, for example, we pray briefly for people in a healing line, perhaps one in fifty will exhibit such manifestations. Afterward, however, twice that many will report that they felt something "lift off" or "depart" at the moment of prayer, even though there were no outwardly observable signs.

By observable signs I mean all kinds of unusual bodily contortions. Some people's limbs become rigid; their hands, for example, may stiffen and become immobile. Other people's bodies will writhe and convulse. Often the person's facial expression will assume an exaggerated look of hatred. A few people roar and growl like animals. Others will speak and may say something like, "*We* hate you." The more fearsome, threatening behavior is rare, while the behavior (such as wailing) showing that the person or spirits are in anguish is more common.

When we become aware that there are evil spirits present, we usually pray on the spot for deliverance. If that brief prayer proves insufficient and more time is needed, we ask an experienced team to take the person to a side room where they can minister to the afflicted individual in some depth. Typically, after we have prayed deliverance for the person, he or she breathes a sigh of relief and rests in the Spirit. The resting takes place only after the deliverance has taken place. Although the person may drop to the floor as soon as we start praying, it is in no sense a "restful" posture until the tormenting spirit has departed.

Sometimes indeed it appears to be the evil spirit itself, rather than the Holy Spirit, who throws the person to the floor. I have observed this especially in Third World countries. The demon fakes the Spirit's power by taking the person out of a healing line before we have a chance to pray with him. It's a false resting intended to prevent ministry from taking place.

One time in Japan, for example, I was praying for people as they came forward. One was a young man about 25 years old. As he approached me, his eyes rolled upward until all I could see were the whites—as if whatever spirits were involved did not want to look at me. It was eerie; the whites of his eyeballs were directed straight at me, yet seeing nothing. He took one more step forward and then, before I could touch him, fell backward. The evil spirits would not let him get near the help he needed, if they could prevent it.

Our understanding is that when there is a strong

presence of God at a meeting, the evil spirits are threatened and have to surface. They are like rabbits hiding in a bramble patch; if the brambles are set on fire, the rabbits come running out. (A disturbing question is why most of our regular church services don't seem to have enough power to flush out these demonic forces!) In the New Testament, it seems that just the presence of Jesus was enough to make the spirits cry out: "What do you want with us, Jesus of Nazareth? Have you come to destroy us?" (Mark 1:24).

When the spirits do surface, they tend to be violent unless we command them to be quiet. In the Gospels we read about demons throwing people to the ground, trying to throw a boy into the fire and various other disruptive activities. They try to injure the person they oppress, as well as to frighten off any onlookers. These same ugly manifestations we sometimes see at our meetings, and they often affect onlookers in the way the demons intend. Most clergy I know want nothing to do with the ministry of deliverance.

When it does happen—for instance, when a person we are praying for starts to shake violently—we should find it a reason for rejoicing rather than retreating. The unseemly disturbance usually means that the Holy Spirit is moving with enough power to rout this particular demonic oppression, and if we can get an experienced team to minister to the oppressed person, in anywhere from five minutes to two hours we will usually see a transformed individual. In consequence, when we minister we like to have several backup teams on hand, because this kind of ministry often takes time. Sometimes the person who falls under God's power is freed without human assistance, but in other cases help is needed.

I would like to add that, while some demonic eruptions are dramatic and fairly obvious, others are not quite so evident. There is, for example, a healthy weeping we often see—an expression of stored-up grief. But occasionally a *spirit of grief* can agitate a person. The external difference is that the demonic agitation is somehow excessive and unnatural. "Excessive" is, of course, a relative term and we need a fair amount of experience to be able to sort out normal human sorrow (which can at times be extraordinarily intense) from demonic activity.

People unfamiliar with this ministry need to understand that the reactions we sometimes see are not directly the work of the Holy Spirit, but are the result of evil spirits resisting the Holy Spirit. Most of the violent response can be avoided, though, if we pray for God's protection before any healing service, commanding any evil spirits that are present to be silent and leave quietly, without disturbance.[8]

Although resting in the Spirit is not necessary at these times, it does seem to provide a setting conducive to Jesus' work of deliverance. It is not the falling, of course, that casts out the spirits; but it is the same power of the Spirit that causes both the falling and the flushing out of the evil spirits, who can't, as it were, take the heat.

In London in the summer of 1975, as I was walking into Westminster Hall where a large conference was taking place, a young woman stopped me. After introducing herself as a fellow American, she asked if I would pray for her inner healing. I explained that there really wasn't time to pray adequately before the next talk began. But as we got into the hall, I noticed a side room and suggested that she and her companion and I step in there and pray briefly in the little time we had. So we ducked into the room and I said a short prayer. She was overcome in the Spirit— much to her own and her friend's surprise—but then she began to tremble and moan. A deliverance had begun. We couldn't stop then, and the ministry took two hours. We came out of the room at the same time the crowd was letting out of the hall. We missed the talk, but she was freed of anxieties and problems that had plagued her for years. Her father, a minister, wrote me three months later to say that his daughter had experienced an extraordinary transformation during the time she rested in the Spirit while we prayed.

David Pytches mentions that a ministry is being developed in the Far East in which the power of drugs is often broken "following a manifestation of the Holy Spirit which has 'prostrated' the addict first."

Drugs provide an obvious doorway, of course, for the entrance of destructive spirits. But sometimes the oppression comes about more subtly. One weekend, for instance, I had ministered to several hundred people in a large Episcopal church. After the very last service on Sunday a young woman in the music group came over and asked me for prayer. She wasn't sure exactly how to pinpoint her problem except that she felt bound up, and that the binding was demonic. She had given her life to the Lord, was baptized in the Spirit and had received much healing, but something was still wrong.

In that setting I had very little time to minister to her, so I simply commanded "any spirit not of Jesus" to leave. After about five minutes of deliverance prayer she rested in the Spirit. A few minutes later she got up and said she felt free. A few weeks later she wrote with her explanation of the deliverance:

> From 1974 until 1984 I belonged to a group which practiced shepherding in the strictest way. I questioned some things, was considered unsubmissive and was subjected to discipline which held me captive until your prayer released me. I was not allowed to have any say; I was not even allowed to cry or show anger. I just had to submit. At one time I had experienced joy and freedom in Christ. After this, no more, ever! And they said they were freeing my spirit! The very first time they counseled me, they imprisoned my spirit. The next time they just increased the bondage. After I left this group an Episcopal priest prayed for me and I received a lot of inner healing. But I couldn't get past this restraint. What your prayer accomplished was this: The Lord went far back and loosed my bound-up spirit, ordering the guards to leave. When the release came, I felt it. It felt so strange to be free, really free for the first time in years!
>
> This release has touched everything in my life. Everything! My music has improved. My appetite is less depraved (I am 100 pounds overweight). Self-esteem has come back! I am free to worship. It's like when I first came to know Jesus and was baptized in the Spirit!

I realize, of course, that much of the strange behavior we observe at our meetings is ambiguous. I mean, how do we know the problem isn't psychological? Why label it demonic?

Early on in my own healing ministry I tended to give a psychological explanation to the things I saw. Then I had some experiences that forced me to reevaluate. One night, for example, I was praying for people one by one in a healing line. As I stopped before a pleasant-looking young woman, her hands shot out and closed around my throat! "We hate you!" she shouted. "We'll kill you!" I had to decide on the spot what to do. "In the name of Jesus Christ," I commanded, "take your hands off my throat!" And she did.

Even in that bizarre situation, I realize there could be a psychological interpretation. The gift of discerning spirits is precisely to help us sort out what is merely on the level of our wounded humanity and what has a demonic source. I know people (my wife is one) whom God has gifted with this discernment, and I find it very helpful—in fact, invaluable—to have such a person by my side when I pray.

I've wondered, too, if the mere mention of possible demonic activity could plant the idea in people's minds so that they may imagine demons when none is there. Yet time after time these episodes occur with no prior exposure to the subject whatsoever.

The following account comes from Jim Hylton who pastors a Baptist church in Texas. At the time this took place (1966) Jim had not seen people fall under the power, nor did he believe in demons. Just previously, though, he had experienced something of the power of the Spirit, which had transformed his preaching. As Jim recounts it:

> One of the ladies in the church was angered by the change she had seen occur in my life. One morning

after a service she exploded, "I hate you. All you want to talk about is Jesus. You were such a good preacher. I am sick and tired of all this Jesus talk."

. . . The next week she came to the study. It was apparent she was no longer angry but broken and apologetic. Her face showed she had lost sleep and experienced much anguish. She wept as she said, "I am sorry for what I said Sunday. You see, the reason I can't stand your speaking about Jesus is because all the sin I have committed brings much anguish to my heart."

I knew little about supernatural power beyond the most supernatural expression of all, the new birth. The Lord knew I was totally incapable to deal with her problem. He simply took me out of it. As I sat in the high-backed chair behind my desk I was suddenly so overwhelmed by the power of the Lord I could no longer hear. I tried to move and found myself plastered to the chair unable to move a muscle. I could see her and knew she was talking but couldn't hear a word. My first thought was I was dying and with the Lord's presence everything else was fading out.

She looked intently, sensing the Lord's power upon me. Then she hurriedly ran out the side exit of the study. As the Lord's power pressed me into the chair I couldn't move. . . . My mind was saying, "I've counseled with many people and this has never happened, Lord. Help me." The intensity of power began to lessen and I heard in my spirit, *Go after her.*

I found her in the auditorium weeping her heart out before the Lord as she repented of every sin He showed her. After she regained some composure I told her I was sorry she was frightened, but I could not explain what was happening. She said, "I understand. It was the glory of the Lord I saw on your face, and I couldn't stand to be there."

We returned to the study, and I sat down in the same chair and was gone again. The power of God came on me until I was barely even able to see this time and could not hear at all. I could see as she fell onto the carpet of the study. After a time which I have no way to measure, she rose to her chair with the glory of God on her. She sat for a long time looking into space saying nothing. My own senses returned to normal, and she looked into my face with a great relief and said, "Demons have gone out of me." A man who didn't even believe in demons had to be taken clear out of the play. For years I never told that story. I never understood it, for one thing. Only in the last year, as I have seen people go into unconsciousness when the power of God comes on them, have I understood what God was doing to me that day.[9]

Although the pastor didn't himself fall to the floor, it is clear he was experiencing the physical powerlessness of resting in the Spirit, even though he had no previous experience of it. Similarly, the woman fell to the carpet of his study—presumably without any previous experience of the falling phenomenon. More extraordinary still, she felt demons leave her, even though Jim (and perhaps she as well) didn't previously believe in them. The psychiatarist Dr. John White comments that "her fall was not the result of mass hysteria since she was alone with a pastor who was incapacitated in his chair. Moreover, she was opposed to behavior of that sort."

This was a classic encounter between the power of God and the forces of evil. Hours of discussion would probably not have wrought such profound changes in the woman's spirit.

In summary, I find that resting in the Spirit is a marvelous *ministry gift* that often leads people to experience the love of Jesus, lasting healing and deliverance.

Evangelists Charles and Frances Hunter reached a similar conclusion about falling under the power (their term for it) after it began happening at their meetings:

> We do not pretend to understand this supernatural manifestation of God's power, but have accepted it as a current demonstration of God's power. The first time it ever happened to us was shocking! While we were praying for a woman at the altar, there came the feeling that she "wasn't there anymore." She had been touched by the power of God and was lying on the floor.
>
> A short time later, this recurred. Again, only once during a service! Then a few months later it happened again. Each time it came as a complete surprise to us. Neither of us felt any special anointing . . . nothing.
>
> Then came February 27, 1973, El Paso, Texas. The power of God fell in a mighty way. The power could be almost heard crackling as a Southern Baptist church had its own day of Pentecost. Somewhere around 100 people fell under the power of God. Probably the most surprised of all the people there were the Hunters. We had never seen anything like this happen in our ministry and certainly couldn't understand it, but we discovered an interesting fact. *God often does a supernatural work in healing, delivering or cleansing while a person is under the power.*[10]

In the early days of their ministry, the Hunters had wondered why so few miracles happened: "We had prayed for probably 10,000 people and only on rare occasions were people healed, maybe ten or twenty, and then we were honestly surprised." It was only later, after they had learned to rely more upon the Spirit, that more healings took place. Then, when the phenomenon of falling under the power began to occur, still more healings followed. So the Hunters understand this phenomenon (as I do) as a sign of the intensity of God's power being present, often accompanied by the power to heal the sick and free the oppressed.

Resting in the Spirit does not indicate that a person is holy—neither the person who falls, nor the minister who is praying. Nor do we need to assume that every revelation a resting person receives is necessarily from God.

It is only by their fruits that we shall know them; but over and over people report that after resting they experience peace, joy and renewed commitment to God. The physical aspects—falling, shaking—are the least important part of it. The theologian Antonio Royo points out that in any case these bodily reactions usually occur only in new Christians. As St. Teresa of Avila observed, "Such experiences, if we use them aright, prepare us to be better servants of God; but sometimes it is the weakest whom God leads by this road; and so there is no ground here either for approval or condemnation. We must base our judgments on the virtues."[11]

4
Between Tears and Laughter

An intriguing pattern emerges when people are overcome in the Spirit:

- A number of people start to *weep;*

- A smaller number start to *laugh.*

In our services most people rest very quietly, but perhaps one out of ten will begin to weep. The Lord is touching griefs that have been repressed for years, enabling them to surface. In other cultures and in other centuries weeping was considered normal. Jesus, for example, wept openly over the death of His friend Lazarus. But we have been taught that men don't cry. From women tears are somewhat more acceptable, but the women most admired today are those whose emotions are most controlled. (Recall the stoic composure of Jackie Kennedy at her husband's funeral.) The path to the healing of our painful past is often through an expression of those pent-up emotions—the tears we needed to let flow but were not able at the time to release.

Experts in the new field of addiction and codependency say that the one basic feeling underlying all addictive problems is *shame,* and that, for healing, the shame has to come out of the darkness and into the light. This is exactly what seems to happen in our healing services: While people rest, the Lord brings the painful memories up out of the unconscious. When this happens, the tears saved for many years finally well up and spill over. Usually, after about five minutes of crying, a deep peace moves in as Jesus touches and heals the wounded past.

The following testimony, written by a woman who had been sexually molested as an infant, is typical of how resting in the Spirit leads to a release of tears, and then to inner healing:

> When you laid hands on me, I rested on the floor. At first I began to cry; then Jesus was there, sitting down. He held out His arms, motioning me to crawl up on His lap. I ran to Him and crawled onto His lap. Once up there He *really* hugged me, tucking my head under His chin. I was 1½ years old—it was after my grandfather had molested me.
>
> Then He showed me what I was like every year from then on. I saw what a precious child I was. Twice I got so fascinated watching me that I'd slip from His embrace and He'd hug me back into His comforting, protecting, loving arms again. I wept both times at His caring and *wanting* to hold me.
>
> At sixteen He said, "Now you know how precious you are"; then I "woke up," so grateful to Jesus. As I walked out of the hall, telling my friends about this, I tried to keep from crying but couldn't.

Perhaps at the time of the original trauma the person needed to be strong—had to be the support for the rest of the family, for example, at the time of a death—and could not allow his emotions free rein. Or perhaps, as in the story above, the damage occurred when the person was too young for conscious recall. Buried down inside over the years, these deep sorrows continue to touch our lives, causing a pervasive sadness we can't shake.

At our services we encourage people to cry, to get the grief out into the light. Because most of us, especially men, have been trained not to cry, we often see people in a healing line shaking with silent sobs they aren't able to let out. So we tell them, "It's all right to cry. Go ahead."

Here is how one woman described the end of a multi-faceted inner healing she received while resting in the Spirit:

> I then became an infant whom Jesus held so tenderly to His bosom. It was at this point that I started to cry, at first softly and hesitantly, and then with deep, wrenching sobs, real bawling. A deep peace came over me at the end of this crying. The crying stopped, just like that. For the rest of the time I was down I felt utterly at peace, a peace broken only when a minister, trying to be helpful, asked the Lord to give me strength to get up.

When someone is able to loosen up and cry, the weeping usually goes on for several minutes as the Lord ministers to him or her. While a professional counselor might try for hours, weeks, sometimes months to surface those past situations that are causing present problems, we often find that Jesus can take people through this whole process in a matter of minutes or hours. Occasionally, though, the grieving will continue after the meeting concludes, as the inner healing progresses. Our friend Dr. Maria Santa-Maria experienced this. The eldest of eight children, she relived her early years as she rested in the Spirit (the Judith in her account is my wife):

> Later, when someone started talking to me, I began to cry. Part of what I was grieving was the loss of my childhood. I had to assume a very responsible role too early in my life, caring for my brothers and sisters.
> Judith walked me to my room. . . . When we got to the room I felt disoriented and tried to pack my suitcase, but I just couldn't do it. I started crying again and we sat down to pray. She asked me what I was feeling and I responded, "It feels as if I'm letting thirty years of grief out of my system."

The sight of people resting and weeping always reminds me of Psalm 56:8, quoted here from the New Jerusalem Bible: "You yourself have counted up my sorrows, [now] collect my tears in your wineskins."

Some tears, of course, come not because of grief, but because we are overwhelmed by the beauty of God's love for us. Here is such an experience:

> Last night, being prayed for by you, I felt myself wanting to open up my heart to love more. I found myself remembering my love for my father, and yet having to turn it off because it was too intense and sometimes having that problem with my husband

and sons. I thought that if I loved too strongly or was too needy, I would scare off the men in my life.

Jesus then appeared and told me I could love Him as strongly as I want, and need Him as much as I want, but that He would always be there for me. I cried and cried.

Then I went upstairs to receive more prayer. On the way I was still crying; I asked Francis and Judith to pray for my heart to open more. I felt myself begin to sway almost as they touched me, and I fought falling over. When it happened again I just surrendered. I remember crying and having people come over and hold me and say, "Jesus loves you." . . . I lay there a long time, feeling drained but peaceful.

The other emotion that can surface in a healing service is joy. When joy is exuberant enough it bursts out in laughter. Laughter is less common than tears at our meetings and usually expresses the wonderful relief of finding oneself free of a long-standing depression or pain. When someone starts laughing—not hysterically, but the deep belly laugh welling up from true happiness—it is really a magnificent experience. Usually the spirit of joy is contagious and soon the whole room is filled with laughter as, one by one, the entire congregation joins in.

I particularly remember one conference for Roman Catholic charismatic renewal in England held at Hopwood Hall in the mid-'70s. At the end of the conference our team was asked to pray a blessing for the six leaders of their National Service Committee. This is a fairly ordinary request and our team started going down the line of leaders as they stood facing the 350 people in the auditorium. When we got to the second person he fell back unexpectedly as we prayed. Then he burst into loud laughter. The same thing happened with the third, fourth, fifth and sixth leaders. They all lay on the platform roaring with laughter, with the soles of their feet sticking out at the audience. Within minutes most of the 350 conferees were dissolved in gales of laughter.

It was a hilarious scene. But not everyone was amused. We were told later that some of the participants from continental Europe went back home in shock. How could an important national religious conference end in such a ridiculous way? After all, most such gatherings end on a note of high seriousness.

Reflecting on it afterward, we decided that laughter was the very best thing that could have happened to close that particular conference. As a people, the English—the culture of the stiff upper lip—needed an unzipped moment of mirthful abandon, a letting go of the tight controls.

Then, too, English Roman Catholics, a once-persecuted minority (Hopwood Hall even boasts a "priest's hole" where priests used to hide), needed a special release from memories of martyrdom, a blessed time of laughter in God's presence.

We laugh when the weight of pain suddenly lifts off, or when a blanket of evil drops away, or when we suddenly glimpse the incredible love and beauty of God—which we have long believed in but perhaps never before experienced.

Typical is the response of one man who was healed of a profound depression:

> As you prayed for me I was slain in the Spirit, and, as I lay on the floor, it felt as if your hand pierced

clear through my body. On the final day of the conference the entire attendance witnessed the depth of my healing as I was enveloped in peals of laughter at our dinner table.

Why Not Anger?

We have come to expect both *tears* and *laughter* at our meetings. But to me it seems significant that *anger* seldom seems to surface when people are resting in the Spirit. When we consider that one of the purposes of counseling is to surface repressed anger, we might expect a lot of it to come bursting forth. But it just doesn't seem to happen that way.

Perhaps this is because anger is not the root emotion, but comes as a result of a far deeper experience of hurt and pain, and it is these roots that Jesus wants to heal. We are angry because we have been deprived of love or treated unjustly. Anger can be dealt with later if it is still there after the pain and hurt have been healed. While people rest in the Spirit, Jesus also often helps them forgive those who have wounded them; this, too, gets at the roots of anger.

At any rate, there must be some significance—spiritual as well as psychological—why God uncovers the wellsprings of grief on the way to healing our wounded hearts. And when the clouds of grief lift, joy follows like the sunshine.

Some sober Christians are shocked when they see people weeping or laughing uproariously at a healing service. I think it would be unnatural if people were being healed by the Lord and there was no crying or laughter to be heard!

Those who sow in tears will reap with songs of joy.
Psalm 126:5

5
Do You Find It in the Bible?

In Scripture we find people falling to the ground in great profusion. But is this the same phenomenon that we observe in our meetings today?

We read, for instance, what happened to King Saul when he was chasing after David to kill him: "The Spirit of God came even upon him, and he walked along prophesying. . . . He stripped off his robes and also prophesied in Samuel's presence. He lay that way all that day and night" (1 Samuel 19:23–24). Here we find the Holy Spirit endowing Saul with a gift of prophecy, and Saul is reported lying on the ground. But what happens to Saul does not seem to be a blessing to him. Rather, it seems God is blocking him from pursuing David and murdering him.

With Saul the falling seems to be similar to what happened to the soldiers sent to arrest Jesus: "When Jesus said, 'I am he,' they drew back and fell to the ground" (John 18:6). Or perhaps Saul's dropping to the earth is like the scene at the empty tomb: "The guards were so afraid of him [the angel] that they shook and became like dead men" (Matthew 28:4).

We have already mentioned that one of God's purposes in knocking people off their feet is to overcome the powers of evil. I have witnessed people who are demonically oppressed unable to remain standing in the presence of God. And occasionally, as I've noted, it seems that oppressed people are robbed of consciousness—removed from the possibility of God's touching and freeing them—not by God, but by the demonic powers themselves.

> When the spirit saw Jesus, it immediately threw the boy into a convulsion. He fell to the ground and rolled around, foaming at the mouth.   Mark 9:20

Clearly it was not God's power knocking this youngster down, but the demonic force trying to take him out of action in order to avoid a confrontation that would end in defeat.

The Bible also records instances, however, of people falling to the ground when no evil is involved, simply by the glory of God. Among many examples we have:

Daniel: "As I listened to him, I fell into a deep sleep, my face to the ground" (Daniel 10:9).

Ezekiel: "This was the appearance of the likeness of the glory of the Lord. When I saw it, I fell facedown" (Ezekiel 1:28).

The beloved disciple, *John:* "When I saw him, I fell at his feet as though dead" (Revelation 1:17).

Peter, James and John: "When the disciples heard this, they fell facedown to the ground, terrified" (Matthew 17:6).

Saul (later *Paul*): "He fell to the ground and heard a

voice say to him, 'Saul, Saul, why do you persecute me?' "
(Acts 9:4).

In all these texts, though, these prophets and apostles
may have experienced something different from what we
see in our meetings:

> 1) Most of them seem to fall *face down*, the normal
> posture of adoration;

> 2) Except for Saul, who was knocked down, they
> may simply have been overwhelmed by God's pres-
> ence, and willingly dropped to their knees;

> 3) There is no imposition of hands.

Cardinal Suenens concludes that

> . . . there is no biblical foundation for the swooning
> brought about by the touch of the healer, in the
> manner of Kathryn Kuhlman. It is important to
> realize that falling to the ground does not always
> have the same significance, and that there is an
> essential difference between falling forward and fall-
> ing backward. Falling forward is a profound, natural
> response which can be motivated by a feeling of
> respect and humility. Falling backward, on the other
> hand, is hardly natural and suggests that the subject
> is, as it were, seized by some alien force.[1]

(In our services, however, we do see some people who
fall forward and others who fall without our ever touching
them.)

To me the most intriguing scriptural reference is 2

Chronicles 5:13–14: "Then the temple of the Lord was filled with a cloud, and the priests could not perform their service because of the cloud, for the glory of the Lord filled the temple of God." Just before this, the priests had all been praising God loudly; then the *shekinah* glory descended. What happened? Was it just too misty and dark to see, or were the priests overcome by the Spirit?

In Dr. Lewis' book about John Wimber's Harrogate conference, he recounts that one of the more common experiences was a feeling of heaviness. One man, for example, felt "a great weight pressing down on my arms and head." He goes on to say that this sensation could not be attributed to suggestion because the speakers never mentioned it from the platform. Furthermore,

> The Hebrew word for God's glory (*kabod*) has a primary meaning of "weight" or "substance." Subsequent investigations have led me to go further than this and to suggest that what is here described could actually be the same kind of phenomenon as that experienced by the ancient Israelites. What has led me to this conclusion has been the mention of a "cloud" or "mist" by a couple of other people in connection with their experiences. . . .
>
> ". . . A grey mist came up . . . covered half a chair, blotted out the dressing table and just a bit of the mirror was poking out of the mist. . . . This was while Jill was worshipping the Lord and his presence was powerful there. So real . . . I couldn't see the furniture through it."
>
> [My correspondent] concluded that this was equivalent to the biblical descriptions of the presence or glory of God which is often perceived as a "cloud." A

close link between this phenomenon—the Shekinah—
and what might be interpreted as the "falling
phenomenon" (especially with reference to the idea
of "weight" as being at the root of the Hebrew word
for "glory") comes in 2 Chronicles 5:13–14, which
reads, "The house of the Lord, was filled with a
cloud, so that the priests could not stand to minister
because of the cloud" (RSV).[2]

If the priests "could not stand," was it because they
were resting under the weight of God's power? I saw
something like this happen during a worship service once
while about fifty of us were celebrating the Eucharist. Ten
minutes into the liturgy about a dozen people fell and
rested peacefully up until Communion time when they
rose to their feet.

What happens physically to people, as I've said earlier,
is never the most important part of this experience. Some
people don't fall, but remain standing or sitting, while
they cease to be overly conscious of what is going on
outside them, so intense is their inner experience. For that
reason Peter's experience on the rooftop is, for me, the
closest Scripture parallel to what we find in our meetings:

> . . . Peter went up on the roof to pray. He became
> hungry and wanted something to eat, and while the
> meal was being prepared, he fell into a trance. He
> saw heaven opened. . . .   Acts 10:9–11

What does the word *trance* describe? Certainly that Peter
experienced a mental state in which he could better
receive the vision that would change the course of Church

history. The text isn't concerned about whether Peter was standing, sitting, kneeling or lying on the roof. The key element is his abstraction from his outer senses so that he could be attentive to God. For me this is the essence of the experience I think of as resting in the Spirit.

6
Rapt in Ecstasy: The Catholic Tradition

When I first saw people overcome in the Spirit in a Kathryn Kuhlman service it seemed very alien to my spiritual tradition. Later, as I began to see it happen when I prayed and the people shared some of their inner spiritual experiences, I was reminded of similar encounters in the lives of the saints down through the ages. The sixteenth-century saint Teresa of Avila, for example, writes in her autobiography:

> While seeking God in this way, the soul becomes conscious that it is fainting almost completely away, in a kind of swoon, with an exceeding great and sweet delight. It gradually ceases to breathe and all its bodily strength begins to fail it: it cannot even move its hands without great pain; its eyes involuntarily close, or, if they remain open, they can hardly see. . . . He can apprehend nothing with the senses, which only hinder his soul's joy and thus harm rather than help him. It is futile for him to attempt to speak: his mind cannot form a single word, nor, if it could, would he have the strength to pronounce it. For in

this condition all outward strength vanishes, while the strength of the soul increases so that it may the better have the fruition of its bliss.

This prayer, for however long it may last, does no harm; at least it has never done any to me, nor do I ever remember feeling any ill effects after the Lord has granted me this favor, however unwell I may have been: indeed, I am generally much the better for it. What harm can possibly be done by so great a blessing? The outward effects are so noteworthy that there can be no doubt some great thing has taken place: we experience a loss of strength but the experience is one of such delight that afterwards our strength grows greater.[1]

Teresa, of course, was an extraordinary saint; yet her description shares many elements of what we find happening to ordinary Christian people (or even notable sinners) at our services:

1) Her body can hardly move;

2) She is not totally unconscious but is aware only vaguely of what is going on around her;

3) Hours can elapse while she is in this condition;

4) The basic thrust of the experience is interior; the body is simply out of it as the person's energy focuses on what is happening in the spiritual realm;

5) Healing and physical well-being are a common result.

I was also reminded of what had happened to ordinary churchgoers through the ministry of John Tauler, a German friar of the fourteenth century.

I had read his story way back when I entered the Dominican Order (Tauler's order) in 1950, and it always stayed with me. John Tauler was a famous preacher in Cologne who noticed one day that a layman had been taking notes on his sermons. When John pressed this man to say what he really thought of his preaching, the layman was reluctant to speak; finally he said that in his opinion John was like the Pharisees of old, who operated more out of pride of intellect than by the light of the Spirit.

John was, naturally, cut to the heart. After an interior struggle, he offered to take the unusual action (especially in that age) of submitting himself to the layman's direction. This man promptly told John to stop preaching and retire to pray and study for a time. When John, the most popular preacher of Cologne, dropped out, his Dominican brothers thought he had gone crazy. One day, as John Tauler was praying, he

> heard with his bodily ears a voice that said: "Stand fast in thy peace and trust in God. And remember that when He was on earth in His human nature, when He cured men of bodily sickness, He also made them well in their souls." The moment these words were spoken, he lost all sense and reason, and knew not whether he was carried away nor how. But when he came to his senses again, he found a great change had taken place in him. All his interior and his outward faculties were conscious of a new strength; and he was gifted with clear perceptions of matters that had before been very strange and alien to him.[2]

The layman's response to this event was significant:

> "I say to thee that now for the very first time thou
> hast been touched by the Most High. And this thou
> must know: as formerly the letter had somewhat
> killed thee, so now shall the same make thee alive
> again. For now thy teaching comes from God the
> Holy Ghost, whereas before it was from the flesh.
> Now thou hast the light of the Holy Ghost, received
> from the grace of God, and hast the Holy Scriptures
> in thee. Therefore, thou hast now a great advantage,
> and in the future far more than formerly thou shalt
> understand the Scriptures, for thou knowest full well
> that the Scriptures in many places seem to contradict
> themselves. But now that in the light of the Holy
> Ghost thou hast received divine grace to possess the
> Holy Scripture in thyself, so wilt thou understand
> that all Scripture hast the same meaning and is never
> self-contradictory."

In short, while John Tauler was what today might be
termed "slain in the Spirit," he was touched by God in an
experiential way for the first time, and received the gift of
understanding.

In time, the layman gave him permission to begin
preaching again—some two years after he had gone into
seclusion and silence. During his first sermon Tauler
started weeping so profusely that he had to stop his
sermon, for which he was further ridiculed by his Dominican brothers. After a while he got up the courage to try
again. This time he preached with such effect that

> When this sermon was over, the Master [Tauler]
> went and offered Mass, but fully forty men stayed

behind in the churchyard, lying as it were in a swoon.
Now the man who had previously given counsel to
the Master, when he learned of this, told the Master
of it, and when the Mass was over he led him to the
churchyard that he might see these people and consider what ailed them. But while Mass was being said
they had risen up and gone away, all but twelve who
still lay there. Then the Master said to the man: "Dear
son, what thinkest thou we should do with these
men?" Then the man went from one to another of
them and touched them. But they moved very little,
and lay there almost as if they were dead. This was a
very strange thing to the Master, for he had never
seen the like before. . . . Then the man said, "These
men are still alive, and I beg thee to have them carried
under shelter, lest by exposure to the night air and by
lying on the cold earth, they should catch cold." And
so the Master had them carried to a warm place.

Later they went to the Master's room where the layman
spoke:

> "Didst thou ever see the like of this in thy whole
> life? Thou now seest plainly what wonders God will
> do by one who is a fit instrument of His work. Dear
> sir, I foresee that this sermon will move many people,
> and they will discuss it one with another. If it be thy
> will, I would advise that thou leave these weak
> children awhile in peace, for they must have a long
> time to deal with this discourse."

Recalling this episode from the spiritual literature of my
own tradition, I was helped not to be totally surprised by

the novelty of it all, but to see that such extraordinary phenomena could happen to ordinary people (the observant layman referred to them as "these weak children").

- The basic purpose of this "very strange thing" was to give the people an *interior* blessing (in this case, to absorb the meaning of the sermon);

- In addition, an *external* publicity purpose was not altogether improper (the people would "discuss it one with another");

- The resting was regarded as a blessing ("Thou now seest plainly what wonders God will do") even though the first reaction had been alarm at the corpse-like appearance of the parishioners;

- These phenomena did not occur until Tauler himself had a spiritual encounter and was filled with a special measure of God's power for ministry;

- The duration of the "immobilization" varied from person to person.

In Catholic tradition when a holy person, a "saint," goes into a trance-like condition, that profound spiritual experience is often referred to as "being rapt in ecstasy." This term has the advantage of referring to both the inner component (experiencing the joy of God's presence) and the bodily component ("rapt" signifying the "carried-away" condition of the body).

Catholic tradition also includes accounts of "falling" due to demonic influence. When another sixteenth-century saint, Ignatius of Loyola, the founder of the

Jesuits, was under investigation by the Inquisition early in his life, one of the accusations directed at him

> was that some of the women under his spiritual direction experienced attacks of melancholy, deep and inexplicable sadness, and fainting spells like epileptic seizures. One of them . . . had been a woman of loose life. Before coming under [Ignatius'] influence, she had relations with a number of students. The phenomena just referred to were much more marked in her. But the others also had similar experiences.[3]

Ignatius readily admitted that five or six of the women under his direction experienced these attacks.

> The cause, so far as it can be understood at all, seemed to be this: these women were reforming their lives; they were abandoning sin or resisting temptations which had come to them from the devil or from their surroundings. The devil was causing this fainting by over-exciting their natural repugnance to a change of life.

At a distance of 350 years it is difficult to say exactly what was going on when these women "fainted," but the author's analysis does seem correct: Demonic forces were battling and trying to stop the women's spiritual progress. This is precisely what we, too, observe occasionally, when the falling phenomenon is caused not by the Holy Spirit but by a resistant alien spirit. In this case, the spirit at work is not hard to discern; the young Ignatius was under no delusion that the epileptic-type seizures were any kind of blessing.

The Catholic Church Today

In today's Roman Catholic Church it is not uncommon for people to rest in the Spirit. One pastor wrote me from New York:

> During the Saturday liturgy at Mt. St. Augustine, Staten Island (Dec. 19, 1976), I was distributing Holy Communion. About 40 persons received from me. Two of them were overcome in the Spirit when I placed the host on their tongues. I was quite surprised, but I didn't think too much about it at the time.
>
> The next day a young man spoke to me about it; he said that all his life he had grave doubts about the presence of Jesus in the host. He was overwhelmed with faith in the Eucharist when he saw the two people fall.
>
> I had never had this experience before, nor have I heard of it before. It was a really unique experience for me.

Some years ago, as I mentioned in the last chapter, I was attending a celebration of the Eucharist where about a dozen persons fell, one by one, without anything being added to the traditional words of the liturgy, and with no one touching them.

Today there are a number of Catholics involved in the healing ministry, priests and laypersons alike, most of whom have seen people overcome by the Spirit in their ministry. Several of the priests are particularly well-known. Father Edward McDonough simply walks down the aisle of the church, sprinkling people with holy water; many of them topple over in the pews without his touching them at all.

Perhaps the best known of all is Father Ralph DiOrio, who conducts large healing services (always with the permission of the local bishop); most of the people he prays with fall under the power of the Spirit.

Consequently, in the Roman Catholic Church today, millions of people are now familiar (at least through hearsay) with this phenomenon. Its validity is often questioned by theologians and bishops and it is certainly not accepted by the Church at large. And yet 25 years ago no one would have even heard of such a thing happening in a Catholic service, much less seen someone "fall under the power" before his very eyes. Clearly we are living in a time of tremendous change!

7
Spreading the Word: The Protestant Tradition

One of the fascinating features of Protestant revival history is the unusual phenomena that almost always accompanied it. "If we insist that revival must be 'decent and orderly,' " writes psychiatrist John White, "we automatically blind ourselves to most revivals. Like the dwarfs in C. S. Lewis' children's story *The Last Battle*, we may spit out heavenly food, for to us it looks like, smells like, tastes like dung and straw."[1]

These revivals were characterized not only by people falling down ("fainting" and "swooning"), but also by weeping, shouting, shaking and all kinds of emotional outbursts. These noisy manifestations resulted in the hostility of the Anglican clergy toward Wesley and, in later revivals, the hostility of other mainline clergy—including the Methodists, the descendants of the Wesleyan revival! Revival has always brought controversy in its wake, and yet these revivals of the eighteenth and nineteenth centuries were what converted people in the English-speaking world. Along with the wild behavior came new life, while the established churches tended to ossify in their pews.

John Wesley (1703–1791)

The most famous of these revival preachers was, of course, John Wesley, an extraordinary evangelist who traveled some 225,000 miles on horseback and delivered some 40,000 sermons! In his desire to reach people and convert them he was the leading proponent of preaching out-of-doors in the fields and squares—for which he was criticized roundly by his fellow Anglican ministers.

It was only in the fourteenth year of his ministry that Wesley started to see people falling over when he preached. Perhaps it began only when, following his painful failures in the newly founded colony of Georgia, he received a special empowering of the Holy Spirit in his famous Aldersgate experience—the strange "warming of his heart" on May 24, 1738, at a quarter to nine. Or perhaps it dates from a slightly later spiritual experience that Wesley describes in his *Journal:*

> Mon., Jan. 1, 1739—Mr. Hall, Kinchin, Ingham, Whitefield, Lane, with about sixty of our brethren. About three in the morning, as we were continuing instant in prayer, the power of God came mightily upon us, insomuch that many cried out for exceeding joy, and many fell to the ground. As soon as we were recovered a little from that awe and amazement at the presence of his Majesty, we broke out with one voice, "We praise thee, O God; we acknowledge thee to be the Lord."

Following these two events, at any rate, the supernatural element in his ministry became more pronounced. For fourteen years it was hardly there; for the next fifty it was!

Noteworthy, it seems to me, is that so much of the swooning occasioned by eighteenth-century preaching was accompanied by convulsions, rather than by the peace that ordinarily accompanies the resting in the Spirit I have seen. Wesley himself identified two causes of the more distressing symptoms:

1) Since his sermons concentrated on conversion, people would naturally cry out and weep;

2) Some people were afflicted by demonic forces and needed to be set free.[2]

Similar manifestations had actually occurred much earlier (1654) when two Quakers, Audland and Camm, preached conversion in Bristol and some of the congregation fell to the ground and foamed at the mouth. But Wesley's ministry became the most celebrated (and controversial) because of the dramatic outbreaks among his audiences.

Here are some descriptions of what happened:

. . . He was preaching at Bristol, to people who cried as in the agonies of death, who were struck to the ground and lay there groaning, who were released (so it seemed) with a visible struggle then and there from the power of the devil.[3]

At Limerick in 1762:

Many more were brought to the birth. All were in floods of tears, cried, prayed, roared aloud, all of them lying on the ground.[4]

At Coleford in 1784:

> When I began to pray, the flame broke out. Many cried aloud, many sank to the ground, many trembled exceedingly.[5]

Even within the Wesleyan revival his colleagues were split on the issue of these boisterous manifestations. One colleague, John Cennick, wrote:

> At first no one knew what to say, but it was soon called the pangs of the new birth, the work of the Holy Ghost, casting out the old man, etc., but some were offended and left the Societies entirely when they saw Mr. Wesley encourage it. I often doubted it was not of the enemy when I saw it and disputed with Mr. Wesley for calling it the work of God. . . . Frequently when none were agitated in the meetings, he prayed, Lord! where are thy tokens and signs, and I don't remember ever to have seen it otherwise than that on his so praying several were seized and screamed out.[6]

Clearly Wesley saw these outbreaks as signs of supernatural power and was worried when they were not present. In his *Journal* he recalled being told one day that James Watson, a well-known backslider, was present at a gathering. Wesley called out, " 'Is James Watson here? If he be, show thy power.'. . . Down dropped James Watson like a stone."[7]

Such dramatic occurrences became common in Wesley's ministry, but toward the end of his long life they diminished, the reason apparently being that once people are converted they don't exhibit the same vehement response as when they first hear the conversion message. It seems that when Wesley would preach in a new city people would swoon away or cry out, but when he returned to that city to preach again, the shouting and fainting would be less in evidence.

Jonathan Edwards (1703–1758)

When Jonathan Edwards accepted the pulpit of the Congregational Church in Northampton, Massachusetts, in 1729, few would have guessed that the mild-mannered young man would become the most celebrated preacher in New England and the leading voice of the first Great Awakening. These Awakenings had a profound influence that is still felt today; the fact that our nation is largely Christian (in name, at least) goes back to these movements. Six of the nine colleges begun in colonial America were the direct result of the Awakenings, as was the enormous Protestant missionary outreach to China, India and Africa.

Edwards, who wrote more than 1,000 sermons, has been stereotyped as something of a wild-eyed fanatic because of his sermon "Sinners in the Hands of an Angry God." Actually, by the standards of his day, he was a calm, reasoning speaker, not a spellbinder. He had a remarkable influence in converting New Englanders and in preparing the way for the English evangelist George Whitefield who came to New England to preach in 1740 and ended his visit with a farewell sermon in Boston to 20,000 people! Whitefield built upon the Awakening started by Edwards and preached four times in Edwards' own church. He visited Edwards' home and was strongly impressed by him ("I think I have not seen his fellow in all New England"), as well as by his family of eleven children and especially Edwards' wife, who made Whitefield wish that he might find a similar woman to marry.

In spite of the emotional outbursts attendant upon some of his sermons, Edwards wanted his preaching judged only by the long-term spiritual effects: "A work is not to be judged by any effects upon the bodies of men, such as tears, trembling, groans, loud outcries, agonies of body, or the *failing of bodily strength*" (emphasis mine).[8]

He points out nonetheless that Scripture does not give us any rule that excludes such effects of preaching upon the body, nor does reason exclude them, "even those that are of the most extraordinary kind; such as taking away the bodily strength. . . ."

Fainting is the word used in these early American revivals for what later came to be known as "falling under the power." Edwards describes the remarkable conversions wrought when Whitefield visited Edwards' hometown of Northampton and says that, on one occasion,

> The whole room was full of nothing but outcries, faintings and such like. Others soon heard of it, in several parts of the town, and came to them; and what they saw and heard there was greatly affecting to them; so that many of them were overpowered in like manner: and it continued thus for some hours; the time being spent in prayer, singing, counseling and conferring. There seemed to be a consequent happy effect of that meeting to several persons, and in the state of religion in the town in general.[9]

After Whitefield's visit these same effects became more pronounced in Edwards' own ministry and, in the following year (1741), when he preached to young people in his home (ages 16 to 26), "many fainted"; some were so overcome they could not walk home but had to spend the night.

Later Edwards invited a visiting evangelist from Yale to speak.

> There were some instances of persons lying in a sort of a trance, remaining for perhaps a whole twenty-four hours motionless, and with their senses locked up; but in the meantime under strong imaginations, as though they went to heaven, and had there a vision of glorious and delightful objects. But when the people were raised to this height, Satan took advantage, and his interposition in many instances soon became very apparent: and a great deal of caution and pains were found necessary to keep the people, many of them, from running wild.

It is interesting, then, to see that the Jonathan Edwards who has come to be regarded as "America's greatest theologian"[10] was well acquainted with people "falling under the power"—while warning at the same time against the excesses of emotionalism and the intrusion of satanic elements on such occasions.

George Whitefield (1714–1770)

What Wesley's revival did for England, his colleague George Whitefield did for the American colonies. Whitefield was the first to be called a "Methodist" by fellow students at Oxford—their mocking term for the group that met for prayer and Bible study, went to church and helped the poor. Even before Wesley, Whitefield was the first to preach to large outdoor crowds in fields and town squares. Ben Franklin estimated that Whitefield could make himself heard by 30,000 people—this in a day before microphones and loudspeakers. In the generation before George Washington, Whitefield was the most popular figure in America.

Early in his career, when he was working with Wesley in England and people started to fall, Whitefield decided to register a protest by letter: "I cannot think it right in you to give so much encouragement to these convulsions which people have been thrown into in your ministry." Ironically enough, when Whitefield came to confront Wesley in person he found himself reprimanded by reality, for when he, Whitefield, was preaching the next day,"four persons sunk down close to him, almost in the same moment. One of them lay without sense or motion. A second trembled exceedingly. The third had strong convulsions all over his body, but made no noise, unless by groans. The fourth, equally convulsed, called upon God, with strong cries and tears. From this time," Wesley writes, "I trust we shall all suffer God to carry on his own work in the way that pleaseth him."[11]

By the time he journeyed to America, Whitefield's preaching was ordinarily accompanied by people toppling over:

> Some were struck pale as death, others were wringing their hands, others lying on the ground, others sinking into the arms of their friends.[12]

> Under Mr. Whitefield's sermon, many of the immense crowd that filled every part of the burial ground, were overcome with fainting. Some sobbed deeply, others wept silently. . . . When the sermon was ended people seemed chained to the ground.[13]

Although the Great Awakening had many preachers, Whitefield, in the estimation of historians, probably had more to do with the wide spreading of evangelical faith and repentance in Christ than any other single person. Between 25,000 and 50,000 people were added to the membership of New England churches during this period. Considering that the population in 1750 was only about 340,000, we can see that some seven to fourteen percent of the entire population was drawn into the Church (especially the Congregational Church) largely through the preaching of Whitefield. In the Middle Colonies the number of Presbyterian pastors more than doubled, while in a twenty-year span Baptist pastors increased from 21 to 79. In the South, the foundation was laid for the great Baptist expansion that came later. Such were the extraordinary fruits of Whitefield's travels, whose preaching was accompanied by people's swooning.

Other preachers, too, witnessed the falling phenomenon. An evangelist friend of Wesley's, John Berridge (described as admirably level-headed), preached with such effect that "great numbers, feeling the arrows of conviction, fell to the ground, some of whom seemed dead, and others in the agony of death, the violence of their bodily convulsions exceeding all description."[14]

Later, at the beginning of the nineteenth century, we read about the revival among the Shakers with trembling, weeping and swooning away, till every appearance of life was gone, and . . . more than a thousand persons fell to the ground apparently without sense or motion. . . . Towards the close of this commotion, viz. about the year 1803, convulsions became prevalent.

Men and women fell in such numbers that it became impossible for the multitude to move about without trampling them, and they were hurried to the meeting house. At no time was the floor less than half covered.[15]

Bishop Francis Asbury (1745–1816)

Born in Birmingham, England, Francis Asbury was appointed by John Wesley in 1771 as a missionary to the Colonies. In his twenties Asbury left England, never to return; he probably contributed more to the spread of Methodism in America than any other person. Traveling by horse throughout the frontier, Asbury was the most celebrated of the circuit riders. It is estimated that he preached more than 16,000 sermons, ordained more than 4,000 ministers, traveled on horseback (or, when he was too old for that, in carriages) some 270,000 miles—wearing out six horses in his lifetime! He never married, never had a home and all that he owned fitted into the two saddle-bags on his horse. He rose every morning at four o'clock, taught himself Latin, Greek and Hebrew, and had a rule of reading 100 pages of good literature a day. His "circuit" was staggering: from Georgia, to Maine, then west to Indiana, when that expanse was still dangerous wilderness.

Clearly Asbury was a disciplined man who likewise

demanded sacrifice and discipline of the men he ordained. He insisted, like Wesley, that camp meetings, even on the remotest frontier, be conducted in a seemly fashion. Yet his revivals, too, were characterized by swooning, shouting, weeping and a kind of wild behavior known as "the jerks."

The Second Great Awakening

As so often happens, Christians grew lukewarm after a generation passed. History records that the next great outpouring of the Spirit, called the "Second Great Awakening," began about the year 1799. Many preachers (notably Peter Cartright) spearheaded the renewal, traveling to the most lawless areas of the then-far-West—Tennessee, Kentucky and the Carolina mountains where murderers, horse thieves and highway robbers had fled to escape the justice of the civilized East Coast. This was the unlikely kind of group gathered for revival at the Red River in Kentucky when "a mighty effusion of God's Spirit came upon the people and the floor was soon covered with the slain; their screams for mercy pierced the heavens."[16]

Then came the famous camp meeting at Cane Ridge, Tennessee, where a frontier crowd estimated at anywhere from 10,000 to 25,000 gathered. To get some estimation of what an extraordinary assemblage this was, we have to realize that Lexington, the largest town in Kentucky, then contained fewer than 1,800 citizens.

The principal preacher was Barton Stone. Another minister, Moses Hoge, described what happened:

> The careless fall down, cry out, tremble, and not infrequently, are affected with convulsive twitch-

ings. . . . Nothing that imagination can paint, can make a stronger impression upon the mind than one of those scenes. Sinners dropping down on every hand, shrieking, groaning, crying for mercy, convulsed; professors praying, agonizing, fainting, falling down in distress, for sinners or in raptures of joy! . . .

As to the work in general there can be no question but it is of God. The subjects of it, for the most part, are deeply wounded for their sins, and give a clear and rational account of their conversion.[17]

Most contemporary clergymen opposed the emotional outbursts at such meetings, and yet it was these revivals that largely contributed to keeping Christianity alive and flourishing in the United States.

What are we to make of the "shrieking and groaning"? I have no difficulty in believing, as did John Wesley, that many of the unseemly outbreaks were due to demonic interference. Then, too, there was an extraordinary emotional component to these gatherings. In these frontier areas people saw no one but their families for months: "The roughness of frontier life, its absence of social controls, and the scarcity of social contacts for those living in isolated cabins, made such people very susceptible to uncontrolled displays when they found themselves in the company of large numbers."[18]

Some of the immense crowd were doubtless lured there simply by the excitement of it all; in that rough throng many brought their booze with them, while one lady of easy virtue set herself up right under the preaching stand until she was discovered and routed out.

Others, however, probably the majority, were sincere in

their desire for changed lives. Especially when preachers concentrated on repentance, those who realized, perhaps for the first time, the seriousness of their sins would burst into tears. Perhaps we, with our staid reserve, are the ones who are abnormal! I remember that in the annals of the Dominican order it was written down as praiseworthy that, in the thirteenth century, townsfolk would walk by a Dominican friary at night and be edified to hear the sobs of the brethren inside the church as they wept for their sins and those of the world.

At any rate, crying and swooning were commonplace at Cane Ridge. One Presbyterian minister (Cane Ridge featured mainly Presbyterian preachers!) counted 3,000 people on the ground at one time. Another observer reported that

> The vast sea of human beings seemed to be agitated as if by a storm. . . . Some of the people were singing, others praying, some crying for mercy in the most piteous accents. . . . While witnessing these scenes, a peculiarly-strange sensation, such as I had never felt before, came over me. My heart beat tumultuously, my knees trembled, my lip quivered, and I felt as though I must fall to the ground. . . . Soon after, I left and went into the woods, and there I strove to rally and man up my courage. . . .
>
> After some time I returned. . . . At one time I saw at least five hundred, swept down in a moment as if a battery of a thousand guns had been opened upon them, and then immediately followed shrieks and shouts that rent the very heavens.[19]

Nearly 200 years later it is hard for us to judge all the factors at work in these camp meetings; it seems that a mixture of forces were at work: There were the hundreds, perhaps thousands, who came to drink and party; there was the hysterical eruption of suppressed emotion; there was probably demonic activity; but also and undeniably there was the genuine power of the Holy Spirit manifested in permanently changed lives.

Charles G. Finney (1792–1875)

In the so-called "Second Phase of the Second Great Awakening" appeared the most famous American preacher of the nineteenth century, Charles G. Finney. Finney was a Calvinist who had studied to be a lawyer and was noted for his logical approach, "like a lawyer arguing before a jury." He had a direct personal style, different from the formal preaching manner of his day. Coming onto the preaching scene in upper New York State in 1824, Finney made it clear that he was opposed to the ranting and excesses of the Kentucky frontier revivals. Finney was a level-headed Presbyterian, concerned about undue emotionalism and conversions that were not rooted in deep conviction.

The first time people were overcome by his preaching occurred one afternoon in Utica, New York, when, fifteen minutes into his sermon, some 400 people fell off their chairs onto the floor. As Finney himself commented later,

> In every age of the Church, cases have occurred in which persons have had such clear manifestations of Divine truth as to prostrate their physical strength entirely. This appears to have been the case with Daniel. He fainted and was unable to stand. Saul of

Tarsus seems to have been overwhelmed and prostrated under the blaze of Divine glory that surrounded him. I have met with many cases where the physical powers were entirely prostrated by a clear apprehension of the infinitely great and weighty truths of religion.

With respect to these cases I remark: that they are not cases of that objectionable excitement of which I spoke in my former letter. For in these cases, the intelligence does not appear to be stultified and confused, but to be full of light. Manifestly there is no such effervescence of the sensibility as produces tears, or any of the usual manifestations of an excited imagination, or deeply moved feelings. There is not that gush of feeling which distracts the thought; but the mind sees truth, unveiled, and in such relations as really to take away all bodily strength, while the mind looks in upon the unveiled glories of the Godhead. The veil seems to be removed from the mind, and the truth is seen much as we must suppose it to be when the spirit is disembodied. No wonder this should overpower the body.

Now such cases have often stumbled those who have witnessed them and yet, so far as I have opportunity to inquire into their subsequent history, I have been persuaded that, in general, these were sound cases of conversion.[20]

The effects of Finney's preaching were extraordinary. According to Lyman Beecher, 100,000 people made a religious affiliation in one year's time, an event unparalleled in the history of the Church. Finney introduced a whole new style of evangelism including such controversial measures (for that time) as praying for persons by name, allowing women to pray and testify, and mobilizing the entire community through home visitations. Of far greater importance, his preaching contributed to profound social reforms such as the abolition of slavery, prison reform and women's rights.

In summary it seems that the preaching in the Protestant Church that has had the most profound and lasting effect in both England and the United States has also been accompanied by listeners being overcome in the Spirit. The greatest preachers in the English-speaking world from the mid-eighteenth century to the end of the nineteenth century all regularly saw people fall over in their services. Among Anglicans, John Wesley; among Methodists, George Whitefield and Francis Asbury; among Congregationalists, Jonathan Edwards; among Presbyterians, Charles Finney and Barton Stone—and of course numerous Quakers and Shakers.

At times in many of these ministries there were other manifestations, such as crying out and shaking, but not always—as in the case of Charles Finney, who apparently witnessed only what we call resting in the Spirit.

It is apparent, too, that most of the evangelists whose preaching was attended by this phenomenon had previously received a special empowering (the baptism of the Spirit). Even Finney, who preached like an attorney pleading his case before a jury, recalled being blessed by an overwhelming experience of God reminiscent of Wesley's, as "waves of liquid love" washed over him—after which his ministry took off!

In the Protestant World Today

The phenomenon of people falling under the power of the Spirit persisted into our century in Pentecostal denominations, but only since the 1960s has it begun to be seen in mainline churches, largely through the influence of the charismatic renewal. (See Reading List, page 183.)

A striking difference is that the falling phenomenon in the eighteenth and nineteenth centuries largely followed upon *preaching,* while today it most often accompanies *prayer for healing* with the laying on of hands. Perhaps this is because in those earlier centuries it was not a common practice to pray for healing. Beginning in the twentieth century, however, falling became prominent at healing services, while almost disappearing at revival meetings featuring preaching, such as Billy Graham's crusades. (There are exceptions, though, like John Wimber's meetings.)

As I mentioned earlier, my first experience of seeing people slain in the Spirit was in Pittsburgh in the late 1960s. Since then I have seen people falling in numerous settings. I have seen it in Catholic gatherings where it is usually quiet and undemonstrative; I have seen it in other places where people react much as they did in the frontier revivals with shaking and weeping.

Such manifestations occur frequently in John Wimber's services. John's ministry is low-key and "laid back" and one of its features is that people in the congregation fall over, usually not while John is preaching, nor while he is praying for them individually, but simply while everyone is waiting in silence after John has asked the Holy Spirit to come. Dr. David Lewis describes a typical Wimber meeting (this one in Sheffield, England):

At the beginning of each so-called clinic session all those present were invited to "wait for" the Holy

Spirit to come upon them. Wimber would pray briefly for the Holy Spirit to "come," then stand at the front while everyone waited quietly, usually standing and often in a position in which the hands were upturned and held out in front as if the persons were in the act of receiving. Some even stood with their hands clasped together behind their backs as if unwilling to participate in what was going on around them. Wimber at the front cracked jokes like, "Now don't get religious on me," but soon began to cry out, "Let it come," as he saw some of the physical manifestations of the Holy Spirit's presence. These ranged from a kind of beatific stillness and quietness settling over a person to the opposite extreme of falling over and lying on the floor. In between there were phenomena such as the shaking of one or both hands, laughing, crying, or a stiffening of the body. Such phenomena have been reported in Christian religious history from at least the time of Wesley onwards, although the biblical reference to the disciples appearing as if drunk on the day of Pentecost might be taken as evidence of similar phenomena in the first-century church.

Most Methodists would be suspicious of such modern phenomena occurring in Methodist churches even if such things occurred at the time of Wesley, and modern Quakers no longer manifest the quaking that gave them their name, but it appears that people of many different denominations at Sheffield experienced such phenomena sometimes involuntarily.[21]

Wimber himself understands these manifestations as the result of a power clash between two kingdoms: the Kingdom of God and the kingdom of Satan. These two kingdoms are not on the same plane, but both are *real* and both wield spiritual power. When they meet there is a real confrontation—a power encounter—often with observable effects.

Like most of the preachers mentioned earlier in this chapter, Wimber was opposed to such goings-on initially. He first encountered them in 1979 when he was pastor of a small church and had invited a guest preacher to address his congregation. As Wimber describes it, the preacher finished his talk saying:

> "Well, that's my testimony. Now the church has been offending the Holy Spirit a long time and [He] is quenched. So we are going to invite [Him] to come and minister." We all waited. The air became thick with anticipation and anxiety.
>
> Then he said, "Holy Spirit, come." And [He] did!
>
> (I must remind you that we were not a "Pentecostal" church with experience or understanding of the sorts of things that began to happen. What happened could not have been learned behavior.)
>
> People fell to the floor. Others who did not believe in tongues loudly spoke in tongues. The speaker roamed among the crowd praying for people, who then immediately fell over with the Holy Spirit resting on them.
>
> I was aghast! All I could think throughout the experience was "Oh, God, get me out of here." In the aftermath, we lost church members and my staff was extremely upset. That night I could not sleep.[22]

But what was the final outcome?

> Over the next few months, supernatural phenomena continued to occur, frequently uninvited and

without any encouragement, spontaneously. New life came into our church. All who were touched by and who yielded to the Holy Spirit—whether they fell over, started shaking, became very quiet and still, or spoke in tongues—accepted the experience and thought it was wonderful, drawing them closer to God. More importantly, prayer, Scripture reading, caring for others, and the love of God all increased. . . .

A revival began that May, and by September we had baptized over seven hundred new converts. There may have been as many as seventeen hundred new converts during a three-and-a-half-month period. I was an expert on church growth, but I had never seen evangelism like that.

Wimber summarizes it all with what I believe is a balanced statement applicable to every church, whether Protestant or Catholic:

Power encounters in the church, in this case without regard for "civilized propriety," catapulted us into all-out revival. What I had thought of as "order" in the twentieth-century church evidently was not the same as what Christians experienced in the New Testament church.

There is a word of caution, though. We would be mistaken to think that lack of order or organization allows the Holy Spirit greater freedom to work, while more order inhibits it. The right kind of order is necessary for the church to develop to maturity and fulfill its tasks. The church is an organism, a living body. A corpse is highly organized, but it is dead—it has no spirit within it. Many congregations are like corpses: well ordered but lacking the life of Christ. On the other hand, the one-celled amoeba, which certainly lacks organization and complexity, has life but can accomplish little. Prayer groups and other Christian organizations that reject the need for leadership are often like amoebas: they have life but are not able to accomplish much.

What God wants is a living body, where the Holy Spirit is free to operate and the body is ordered in such a manner that it can accomplish much. This body is quite complex, because the goal of evangelism and discipleship is an involved process. A key, though, is that God's order—not our own—be established. Sometimes he tips over our order so he can establish his.

8
Objections

In 1978, I had a two-and-a-half-hour interview in Rome at the Sacred Congregation of Faith and Doctrine (known in earlier years as the Holy Office, and still earlier as the Inquisition) where Archbishop Jerome Hamer, the acting head of the Congregation, questioned me extensively on five areas of my teaching on healing. It was not a formal inquiry, nor was I subject to any kind of accusation. The interview came as a result of several church leaders' reports that (as is usual with anything new) complaints and letters had been addressed to the Vatican and that it would be helpful for me to appear and explain what I was teaching.

One of the five sections of my interrogation—each one a half hour in length—was on "slaying in the Spirit." The Archbishop's main question was: Isn't it just a psychological phenomenon—an effect of mass hysteria such as happens to teenagers at rock concerts when they swoon in the presence of their idols? Clearly, whoever funneled the complaints to Rome believed that our healing services were American nonsense with about as much Christian content as a Beatles concert. And just as clearly, the Church does not want to encourage mass hysteria and emotionalism as a replacement for the true Gospel, which emphasizes sacrifice and rational commitment.

My defense was simply that our meetings were generally peaceful and very quiet; that resting was something that simply happened, not something I manufactured; and that people's lives were often changed by the experience. (I should add that the result of this extensive discussion was favorable: Archbishop Hamer, who was courteous and affable, commented that I had raised persuasive points.)

A year later, however, in a booklet on ecumenism, Cardinal Suenens addressed the subject under the heading of "Parapsychological Phenomena." Among other things, he wrote:

> The expectant interior dispositions of the person who is open to the experience can explain the subjective feelings he has, without looking for a supernatural explanation.
>
> We must unite ourselves with all the bishops who caution against emotionalism and "supernaturalism" and ask the leaders of the renewal to avoid all situations in which these manifestations become mass phenomena or a public spectacle. . . .
>
> We appeal to the leaders of the charismatic renewal to exercise great caution and not to induce these phenomena by the way they pray with people.[1]

Cardinal Suenens' clear implication is that the minister somehow brings about the falling. Earlier, in fact, at the Second Roman Catholic International Conference on Charismatic Renewal, held in Dublin, Ireland, in 1977, Cardinal Suenens called me into his room and told me to stop the practice of slaying in the Spirit, as if it were something that I was doing purposely. I was not, of course, nor was I sure how we were supposed to "avoid all situations" in which these manifestations become a public spectacle, unless we simply avoided praying with people in public.

The objections that Cardinal Suenens and other authors bring up, on the other hand, are real. Let's take them up one by one.

Shamanism

The criticism I personally find most painful is when what happens at our meetings is compared to shamanism or witchcraft. It's like saying that since witch doctors perform rituals to heal the sick, Christians should not hold healing services.

The *source* of the power, however, is totally different: In one case it is God, and in the other, Satan. The way to avoid the difficulty is really very easy: If the minister is a Christian who turns to God, the ministry will not be satanic. The person and intention of the minister are all-important in determining what spirit is operative. At our meetings we sometimes see demonic eruptions, but, as I have said, these outbreaks are the response of evil spirits to the power of the Holy Spirit; they would not occur if the power of the Holy Spirit were not there, threatening them with expulsion.

Fraud

A magician who calls himself "the Amazing Randi" has made a career out of exposing fakes. In his book, *The Faith*

Healers, Randi attacks Christian healers, some of whom he does indeed expose as frauds. In particular, certain ones have simulated the word of knowledge, employing confederates who discover information about sick people and pipe it to a tiny transmitter in the healer's ear, who thereupon "miraculously" receives it in the pulpit.

In regard to slaying in the Spirit he alleges that several of the evangelists he investigated tried to push him or his confederates over. I can readily believe this: I persistently hear reports from friends who have attended services where evangelists seemed so eager to manufacture results that they simply gave people a shove!

Such procedures are not only reprehensible in themselves, but cast an ugly pall over what is, for those of us who have witnessed the real thing, one of the most winning manifestations of God's love: His desire to make us whole. (I do not know how Randi explains it when people fall without being touched.)

Again, everything depends on the character and intention of the minister of healing. For the sake of all of us who care about this ministry, we must be wise to the ways of charlatans.

The Power of Suggestion

The most frequent objection to resting in the Spirit is that it may merely be the result of autohypnosis (on the part of the person being prayed for) and playing upon people's suggestibility (on the part of the minister).

The psychological factor of suggestibility will always be involved whenever people are involved, and resting in the Spirit is no exception. To say, on the other hand, that a psychological dimension is present does not mean that this dimension is necessarily bad. When pastors preach they are trying to persuade, and the element of suggestibility is bound to play a part, even though the Spirit of God should do most of the convincing.

There is necessarily, as in all things human, a *mixture.*

In our day, some Scripture commentators believe that Jesus' healing ministry was based entirely on the power of suggestion. They write something like: "The man suffering from hysterical lameness heard Jesus' powerful suggestion, 'Stand up and walk,' threw away his crutches and walked. He was dramatically healed of his imaginary disease and the simple people were amazed."

And who is to say that some healing that goes on in our services does not take place in this way? I will never forget a conversation I had with a Jewish friend who said, "I have no problem believing that people are healed at your meetings. After all, thirty percent of medical patients are healed through the placebo effect, when their doctor prescribes a sugar-coated pill and tells them it's going to heal them. You are a charismatic figure and people believe you can heal them. You are simply a living sugar-coated pill and thirty percent of the people who come to you will be healed. I have no problem with that. More power to you, if you can do it. That is what you're talking about, isn't it?"

I told him that wasn't what I was talking about. Some people were, no doubt, healed through suggestion, but usually something more was involved: the power of God. An hour later I prayed for his daughter who had suffered a (very real) physical injury to her hip and leg as the result of an auto accident. In a five-minute prayer she was almost totally healed. I believe that convinced my friend that spiritual healing is more than the placebo effect!

Psychological factors are unavoidable. To mention the possibility of resting in the Spirit before a service and to have catchers in evidence during prayer are obviously factors of suggestion. The question is: Are they excessive? Are they used to manipulate people?

In any case, resting in the Spirit cannot be due altogether to the power of suggestion, since people so often fall without ever having heard about it before. Just in today's mail I received another such account from John Evans, a university professor, who also helps lead a Christian community:

> About fifteen years ago, a retired priest attended our prayer meetings regularly. He did so because of affection for us and, in part, because he had anxieties about renewal enthusiasm and spirituality. In part, too, because he had crippling arthritis which kept him in constant pain. (Occasionally, he would call out some criticism or caution during the meeting. That was fine with us, because he was fine with us.)
>
> One night we were having a core meeting and Father asked for prayers because he had not been able to sleep for several nights due to his pain. Immediately we prayed for him and he quickly fell asleep. We were not familiar with resting in the Spirit so we just kept on praying, happy that our prayers seemed to bring peace and sleep so quickly. Then we went on with the business of the night. When we noticed that Father hadn't awakened after an hour of sleeping in his chair, we were concerned. We tried gently to rouse him. He kept on sleeping. Then we

spoke loudly, "Father, wake up." He kept sleeping. By this time we were worried. So we called a nurse who was a member of the team and she came with some vials of ammonia. She cracked two or three vials under his nose with no results. Then she checked his vital signs, which were normal. She wasn't worried, but we were, so we called for his doctor and an ambulance to take him to the hospital. We followed and arrived at the same time as the ambulance. Almost immediately after being put in one of the beds in the emergency room, Father woke up and said, "That was the best sleep I've had in weeks." He was checked and discharged.

We didn't know much about such things, as I said, and we were sure that Father would not have appreciated our telling him that he had been "slain in the Spirit" (to use the language current then) so we said nothing to him about the night's events. Among ourselves, we wondered, of course, "if Father had been slain in the Spirit." As time went on, I had no trouble believing in the reality of the Lord's caring for people in this way because of that early experience with Father, a person who knew nothing about the phenomenon and was in no way inclined toward anything which would have seemed to him to smack of religious enthusiasm.

Interesting, too, is the research of the social anthropologist Dr. David Lewis, previously mentioned, who analyzed 1,890 responses from people who had attended John Wimber's Harrogate conference. He came to the conclusion that the unusual phenomena occurring there were not due primarily to the power of suggestion:

1) The respondents themselves felt this was not the case: Only *one* of the nearly two thousand who answered his lengthy questionnaire believed that suggestion had caused her to fall.

2) Analyzing the personality types of those who experienced spiritual phenomena (resting in the Spirit was only one of these), Lewis found that *no particular psychological type* was more susceptible than any other. Those ranking high on extroversion and neuroticism scales, who would be the most likely candidates for mass hysteria, were no more likely to manifest this behavior than anyone else. Quite the contrary. "Those ranking *low* on the neuroticism scale report the 'falling phenomenon' much more often than do those ranking high on the neuroticism scale."[2]

3) As for the possibility that the evangelist produces a state of heightened suggestibility, Dr. Lewis points to the casualness of Wimber's speaking style, the frequent breaks for refreshments and the lack of hype before the times of ministry.

4) Lewis lists more than 200 different classifications of spiritual phenomena that people experienced at Harrogate. Most of them were not mentioned at all in the teaching; some of them were opposites—some people couldn't move while others shook; some felt that areas of their bodies were hot, others felt waves of cold. Of the 1,890 respondents, 355 reported falling down. Here it is fascinating to note that of those who had fallen in previous conferences, 69 percent did not

fall at Harrogate. It can hardly be argued, therefore, that this is a learned behavior. In fact, there appears "to be a progression over time from the more dramatic to less dramatic phenomena in the experience of certain individuals. This appears to be linked with a belief that various problem areas have been sorted out in the more 'dramatic sessions.' "[3]

Sensationalism

People being what we are, we tend to look for the novel and spectacular. Instead of looking for Jesus, we want observable results. And when people are falling over right and left, a circus atmosphere can result that would bother any reflective Christian. Last year, after one meeting in which a woman evangelist seemed to take delight in seeing people fall, a Jewish observer told me that it all seemed like witchcraft to her. Newspapers don't help either; reporters naturally tend to pick out noteworthy externals and pass over more subtle and inward happenings. I don't blame writers for looking for what is dramatic and can be described in visual terms, but it is easy for balance to disappear, both at the meeting itself and in any description of the meeting read afterward by those who were not there.

Sensationalism is a problem, therefore, that isn't going to go away. Yet I have found that once people become familiar with seeing people fall over, they simply don't pay that much attention to it anymore. Time takes care of the problem; it becomes a matter of course! It's very much like tongues-speaking; in the early days of charismatic renewal, it was a sensation with everyone asking, "Have you prayed in tongues yet?" Many feared it would cater to spiritual pride, with those who didn't pray in tongues made to feel spiritually inferior. Critics pointed out, furthermore, that many of those who prayed in tongues were spiritually immature: "Tongues-speaking teaches childish Christians to look for spiritual externals instead of concentrating on the long, disciplined Christian walk that leads through suffering to true union with God." Such cautions had validity. But the overreaction (suppress tongues) was dead wrong; it didn't allow for the purpose of praying in tongues for beginners—an encouragement given to help them on the way.

In the course of time, people got used to tongues and eventually the phenomenon took its rightful place; today you hear little about it. It has come to be accepted as an ordinary, albeit supernatural gift of God.

So it should be with resting in the Spirit.

Vulgarity

Although people seldom admit it, I believe the deepest prejudice of all against being overcome by the Spirit is a fear of appearing vulgar—in its root meaning, being a member of the common class of unwashed humanity. In this case, it could represent those Christians who are theologically unlearned—the crowd that meets in tents to wave their arms. It is the response of the religious leaders of Jerusalem, who scorned Peter and John—even after they had performed a healing miracle—as ordinary, unschooled laymen (Acts 4:13).

The ridiculous spectacle of falling over, with everyone there to watch, is a demeaning prospect—something like slipping on a banana peel. No dignified, self-controlled person would want that to happen, much less in the sanctified precinct of a church! Especially in Europe I feel a real hostility to the idea of resting in the Spirit. It is as if they consider it a typical American innovation, a show-biz import, representative of the shallow spirituality of TV evangelism.

I can certainly appreciate that reaction. I received a letter recently from a knowledgeable friend in Europe who wrote in regard to theologians who are justly unhappy with the falling phenomenon:

> I suspect the reason for this was the ways in which the ministry was conducted in certain parts of Europe when it became the latest fad to sweep the Renewal. Here in Italy there are some groups that encourage people to "stay under the power" as a definitive sign of the presence of the Holy Spirit. There are mighty strange things done around the world in the name of God, as you well know.

So there needs to be a balance, and I agree with all those critics who cry out for it (although we may disagree as to where that point of balance lies).

But is it also possible that God occasionally wants us to be clowns for His sake—to be willing to appear a bit ridiculous and take ourselves less seriously (as with the English leaders who fell over at the end of their conference)? Maybe our dignity and decorum have to go. Maybe, as G. K. Chesterton advocated, Christianity needs to stand the world on its head. And Christians should set the example; maybe that's why people are falling over these days!

I do know that our desire to be fashionably accepted by our society is weakening, if not killing, Christianity in the First World. As we have seen, many of the great Christian revivals were characterized not only by people's repentance, but by their acting in ridiculous ways, while respectable church leaders were standing on the sidelines, muttering criticisms.

Psychiatrist John White observes:

> Revivals spawn their own leaders. Then comes a general bristling of whiskers among the old guard and its supporters. There are two sources of discontent. First, the clergy-laity distinction becomes blurred, threatening clerical institutions. Second, emerging leaders may lack formal training and social polish. . . . Whenever the kingdom advances, the front line is perceived as scum. There is a sociological as well as a spiritual explanation of this. Christian movements have proved to be powerful in the degree that they have captured the hearts of the poor—for God goes for the rabble. Thus the new breed of Christians generally includes a disproportionate number of people seen as the social inferiors of the religious establishment. There are exceptions to the rule, but in general Anglicans and Presbyterians regarded early Methodists as Johnny-come-latelies. North American Methodists in turn could look down on Pentecostals, not only for their doctrine and practice, but for the social origins of their members, drawn as they often were from the lowest ranks of society.[4]

Dr. White further brings out that most educated people in our Western world are very uncomfortable with their own emotions—and other people's as well: "To this day, psychologically sophisticated as I may be, I feel uncomfortable with people who emote too much around me."[5]

Thus I suspect that fear of vulgarity is behind much of the resistance to resting in the Spirit:

1) Because the phenomenon is associated with tent-type Pentecostals—a spiritual underclass;

2) Because weeping and other emotional outbursts may accompany being overcome in the Spirit, and such things are embarrassing;

3) Because church demands our "best" behavior.

Perhaps the quiet decorum of our churches reflects a meditative sense of awe in the presence of God. But if the stillness is never broken by tears or laughter or cries of joy, it may also indicate that our lives are not being changed. In short, shouting and laughing may indeed reveal a superficial American spirituality of "cheap grace." But if there is only silence, perhaps that, too, can reflect a surface Christianity, where nothing changes and the congregation's social status quo is never threatened by revival.

"Unworthiness" of Recipients

A less frequent objection—but a strongly held one—is the reverse of the "vulgarity" complaint: If people who fall are recipients of a divine blessing, then, the argument goes, they should somehow "deserve" to be singled out in this way. But it is not at all rare for the newest, least-committed Christian to experience this phenomenon!

Those who raise this objection don't like our comparing what happens to people at our services with the spiritual encounters of the saints, holy people who came to these deep spiritual experiences after many years of discipline and prayer. It would certainly be wrong to equate the spiritual maturity of the saints with the sometimes manifest immaturity of beginners in the spiritual life who are touched by the power of God at our meetings. But if these experiences are graces, gifts to help people along, why shouldn't beginners receive a transforming experience at the very start of their Christian walk—as did the apostle Paul—to shake them out of their past life and start them on their way toward becoming new creations?

Are these gifts, or are they the earned rewards of service? By definition they are gifts. Do we hear an echo of the elder brother in this critique, complaining that the Father is having a party for a Prodigal Son who hasn't paid his dues?

Problems of Proof

A final objection is that you can't *prove* that any given blessing resulted because a person rested in the Spirit. This, too, is an accurate observation; you can't prove much from any individual experience.

I first ran into this problem some twenty years ago when speaking to a group of medical students in Memphis, Tennessee. I was sharing with them some particularly striking testimonies of healing that I thought would convince them of the power of God to heal through prayer. The doctor who had convened the meeting responded, *"Post hoc, non propter hoc."* (I had not heard that Latin phrase since seminary: *"After this, not because of this."*) You cannot prove that the healing came about *because* you prayed. All you can say is that the healing happened *after* you prayed. Something other than your prayer may have caused the healing.

Logically, of course, he had me.

Five years later, in 1975, I attended a meeting sponsored by the staff at the celebrated healing shrine at Lourdes. The French physicians on staff at Lourdes expressed the same helplessness that I had felt in the face of this argument: They had a hard time proving medically, to the satisfaction of the theological board, that any given healing was supernatural. Thousands of healings take place at Lourdes every year, but only about once every two years can they certify that a miracle has taken place, a healing that God's power alone, not nature, could account for. Some of the doctors felt they were spinning their wheels with an impossible task of proving supernatural causation. (And the doctors found it harder to convince the theological board than the medical board!)

One approach to the issue is simply to take an inventory of hundreds of cases (the inductive method of proof), rather than singling out any one experience and trying to prove anything by it. If hundreds of people say they experience blessings and healings while resting in the Spirit, and positive, lasting effects follow in their lives, then resting seems to be a favored situation for God's work.

It seems to me, consequently, that the best way to evaluate resting in the Spirit is to speak to as many people as possible who have experienced it.

This seems to be exactly what those who raise this

objection refuse to do. Four years ago we conducted a five-day summer conference for 300 people; during one healing service many people rested. The auditorium where we met was open all the way around and, unfortunately, some people attending another conference wandered in halfway through this service. They were all professional people, a minister and several educators, appalled by what they saw: people lying on the floor, a few of them crying out. Most of the noise came from five people who were being freed of demonic oppression. The next day this irate group of onlookers accosted Judith and me outside the dining hall and accused us of provoking psychotic breaks and leaving people unattended after we had stirred up their psychoses. (Actually, team members had been ministering to those in need of attention.)

We tried to explain that these were not psychotic breaks but simply the angry response of demons to the power of the Spirit. We proposed what we thought would appeal to any rational person: "Have you talked today to any of these people you claim were traumatized?" Already two of these supposed victims had told us in the dining hall that they felt transformed by what had happened the night before. We offered to find the five who had been in pain the previous evening so that the outraged observers could interview them.

But they would not do it. Instead, they went the next day to the director of the conference center and reported that Judith and I had placed our fingers on people's jugular veins and pressed down until they went unconscious! I share this only to indicate the strong reactions triggered sometimes by a first encounter with this phenomenon.

*   *   *

Clearly, in all this, problems arise principally because the falling phenomenon appears so sensational and people understand it so little. Again, like the gift of tongues when it was new to most of us, people are impressed, favorably or unfavorably, because it is so different. I hope that when resting in the Spirit is better known, its spiritual purpose will become central, and it will no longer cause astonishment. But the answer to most of these objections is not suppression—in which case its value and purpose are lost to the community—but its wise use until it becomes so well understood that its sensational aspects are minimized.

Once more the testimony of psychiatrist John White is particularly relevant:

> For my part I am glad that God ignores our petty notions of propriety as he deals with men and women. I want God to be God. But because I suffer from a skeptical disposition I have to see for myself what is happening, to inquire, to test. . . .
>
> Having therefore seen and examined carefully, I am convinced that while some manifestations represent psychological aberrations, and others demonic fear and protest, many and perhaps most of the manifestations evidence the presence in power of the Holy Spirit. . . . Your fall and your shaking may be a genuine expression of the Spirit resting on you. But the Spirit may not benefit you in the least if God does not have his way with you, while someone who neither trembles nor falls may profit greatly.
>
> Surely it is fruit that matters.[6]

9
Who Falls and Who Doesn't?

I think it is a real blessing to be the kind of person who is easily overcome by the Spirit. I say this objectively, because I do not seem to be that kind of person, and I have yet to receive the kind of in-depth experience I see other people having.

It is claimed that easily suggestible people are the most likely to fall, and in part this may be true. As noted, some of what we see can probably be put down to the power of suggestion, emotionalism and all that. Being suggestible is generally seen as a weakness. And if we convince ourselves it is mostly the weak-willed, overly emotional types who fall over, then clearly we won't want to be among them.

I see it in a different way: I believe that people who are more *open* (as opposed to closed personalities) are more likely to rest. Persons determinedly self-controlled are not nearly so likely to be overcome by the Spirit. When a person comes forward for prayer with compressed lips and a tight jaw, I am surprised if he falls. It is good, of course, to be disciplined; I am just saying that someone who has a joyous, open spirit seems more likely to rest than an overly controlled, super-serious person. Generally it's a plus, not a minus, to be the kind of person who rests easily in the Spirit.

I have also noticed that artistic, creative, intuitive people seem more likely to fall than rational, intellectual types. When people in the music ministry, for instance, come forward for prayer, they are more likely to rest in the Spirit.

In general, more women than men seem to experience resting, perhaps by a two-to-one margin. Is it that women in our society are more in tune with the spiritual? Are they more likely to admit their dependence on God?

When church leaders characterize the person who falls back as "emotionally immature," I am forced to ask, Do men have a constitutional dislike for such phenomena because we tend, as a group, to be overly controlled ourselves, and fear anything that smacks of letting go? I think, as human beings, and even as Christians, we "professionals" are apt to seek our security through keeping a tight grip on the reins. We are afraid of the unpredictable. Deep down we prefer law to grace, control to freedom.

Think, judge, then act has been the rule for most of my life. Anything I don't understand, anything that implies that my feelings are influencing me is something I have learned to mistrust. Only now am I beginning to open up more, to try to listen to the Spirit, to leave Ur of the Chaldees like Abraham and venture trustingly into uncharted territory.

As Dr. John White remarks:

> Our personalities tend to determine the form in which we react to anything. The same verse of Scripture will be received by one person with enthusiasm, by another with anxiety, by yet another with suspicion. Some people are open, others more closed, some more responsive, others more controlled. . . . It should not surprise us, therefore, to find that people's responses to close contact with the Holy Spirit's power may vary.[1]

Some people are really afraid to let go. It isn't so much a spiritual problem as an emotional one; they are ill-at-ease with anything they can't program and predetermine. They may seem to be mature, but they have lost their ability to respond to life with spontaneity.

If I could characterize the kind of person least likely to fall (admitting that I have encountered exceptions), he would be an elderly man of Anglo-Saxon or Germanic ancestry who had a hard childhood with very little play. Probably he had to take responsibility early in life; he grew up in a church that emphasized discipline and self-denial; and his present profession demands strict accounting. Now, all these qualities are virtues. It's just that they need balance.

The most likely to rest would be a young woman of Latin American or African ancestry, of artistic bent—perhaps a singer—whose childhood has been filled with games and laughter. Perhaps she has experimented with drugs; she may have many sins to repent of in comparison to our solid German type. Yet she is more likely to fall, and it is precisely while resting that she may receive a marvelous, surprising grace of conversion and repentance.

In short, resting in the Spirit is not a reward for virtue, nor is it a sign of hysteria. It is simply an occasion when grace may be poured out, especially to those who are free to let go of their conscious controls.

Those who are closed to the experience, on the other hand, and do not want it may also fall. Like an angry Saul, they are struck down unexpectedly on the road to Damascus.

Such a skeptic was our friend Dr. Maria Santa-Maria, a psychologist.

Resting in the Spirit was one of the factors that kept me away from the charismatic renewal. I had attended a couple of retreats and conferences. When people would go forward for healing prayer and start falling, my defenses would immediately go up. I would become very self-conscious and analytical about this "resting in the Spirit" phenomenon.

As a professional counselor, I knew the power of suggestion. As a matter of fact, in 1968 when someone laid hands on me for the baptism of the Holy Spirit, I received the gift of tongues. However, I consulted a priest psychologist friend of mine, who told me that if I could "turn it on and off like a water faucet" it was auto-suggestion and not supernatural. I believed him, and even though I had experienced a deep personal sense of being loved by God as never before, I discounted the whole experience.

Ten years later, my friend Judith Sewell (now Judith MacNutt) invited me to attend a conference led by Francis MacNutt, at Mt. St. Augustine in Staten Island, New York. Very reluctantly, I agreed to go.

The day after the conference ended Francis had devoted time to pray for healing with local people in the chapel. After he finished, someone suggested we pray for him for a renewal of his energy, since he was going on to New Jersey to speak at another very large conference. About ten people gathered around him as he sat on a chair.

Somehow I ended up holding Francis' right hand. As we prayed, I began to feel this tremendous surge of energy gently pushing me over. I said to myself: *This shouldn't be happening now; it's Francis we are praying for, not me.* I intentionally set my feet wider apart in order to prevent myself from falling. But the energy flow continued gently pushing me backward. I just decided to stop fighting and go with it.

Someone gently laid me on the floor as I went backwards. I remained there for a few minutes in a semi-conscious state. It felt very peaceful. When I opened my eyes Francis smiled and said: "You stole all my blessings." I responded: "If that's what happened, I'll take it."

Others I know who have not been overcome when they were prayed for seem to be very close to the Lord. Perhaps the reason such people do not fall is that they are already so accustomed to the power of the Spirit that there is very little differential in power, as it were, between the indwelling presence of God and what flows in through prayer. St. Teresa of Avila observed that when she grew more accustomed to the power of God, the bodily manifestations became less, while her prayer life became stronger.

Thus, I think it is foolhardy to make a general judgment about people who are overcome in the Spirit as distinct from those who are not. Some fall because they are immature and just looking for some kind of experience; others refuse to fall because they are emotionally restricted (and immature in a different way). Some people are overcome by the Spirit because they are open and yielded to the Spirit; others don't fall because they are already so close to God, so used to God's presence, that there is no reason for them to fall. And some who, I believe, are very close to the Lord and sensitive to the inspirations of the Spirit often rest in this way at our meetings.

As always, we should be wary of judging others lest we ourselves be judged!

10
To Sum Up

I believe there are two components to resting in the Spirit.

The first element is *physical*, external, the falling phenomenon. To concentrate solely on bodies falling does an injustice to what we see happening in our prayer meetings.

The second element is *internal*, the intense preoccupation of our spirit with the presence of God. Although this does not happen to everyone—nor perhaps even to most people who rest in the Spirit—it does happen to a significant percentage, who then experience great blessings. These include knowing Jesus better and loving God more; receiving an intense love of prayer and desire to study Scripture; receiving deep inner and physical healings; and being delivered from demonic bondage.

These are, of course, benefits all Christians seek, and often we receive these gifts without falling in the Spirit. And it is true that many people fall without much of anything happening on the inside. But it is helpful when the person falls and rests; in this relaxed condition, he is better able to experience the presence and blessings of God. The falling and resting are not necessary, but as a *means*, they can be helpful.

The only ultimate test I know for the value of resting in the Spirit is Christ's own: "By their fruits you shall know them." When we hear of the marvelous transformations of lives . . . of the healings . . . of the freeing from lifelong bondage repeated in thousands of lives, I am overwhelmed with gratitude at seeing how God's compassion has reached out to touch our poor, weak, broken humanity.

I long for a day when resting in the Spirit is not seen as some weird, fringe element in Christianity, but as a normal—even ordinary—component of prayer meetings.

Dare we hope for a return to the time, two hundred years ago, when Methodist authorities suggested that if listeners fell to the ground while a Methodist evangelist was preaching, it was considered the best sign that he was called to be a bishop?

Part II

If It Happens When You Pray . . . Notes to Those in the Healing Ministry

11
The One Who Does the Praying

When we get involved in praying for people, we may find, as I did, that we start to see people overcome in the Spirit. Then, as we notice certain patterns to this occurrence, we realize there must be a meaning behind the various experiences. Curious as I am, I have always delighted in sitting down and learning from people in the healing ministry. In this part of the book, then, I want to share with you what I always want people of experience to share with me—what they have learned by actually praying with people.

The most important thing, of course, for those of us who pray for healing is to try to keep our motivation pure—in every aspect of this ministry. This can be especially hard if, during our prayers, people begin falling over: Our egos can become involved with this seeming evidence of God's anointing on our endeavors! I frequently get reports from people who say they were pushed over by this or that healing evangelist. The actions of a few tend, regrettably, to discredit the whole phenomenon of resting in the Spirit. Magician James

Randi, in the book mentioned previously, writes about one such evangelist:

> He also does the "slaying in the spirit" demonstration, to which I subjected myself at his meeting. I stood before him and two huge "catchers" stood at my sides. He placed one hand at the small of my back, pressed the other to my forehead and easily pushed me over. Kurtz was not such a "pushover." He decided to resist, and though [the evangelist] pushed him hard three times, Kurtz remained firmly standing. Disgusted, [the evangelist] went on to more pliant victims.[1]

I myself have observed some Pentecostal preachers who end their prayer by giving a little shove on the forehead, enough to push an unresisting person over.

In Jamie Buckingham's fascinating biography of Kathryn Kuhlman he shares, with his typical honesty, how toward the end of her life she sometimes lacked spiritual power. One time she had Jamie up on the platform leading the singing:

> Kathryn was moving back and forth across the stage, saying all her favorite phrases. They seemed empty. The singer had climbed to her feet and Kathryn touched her again (earlier she had touched the singer who fell to the floor). Nothing happened this time. In a desperate move I heard her say, "The Spirit is all over you, Jamie." She swept toward me, putting her hand on my jaw as I sang. There had been times in the past when, if she even got close to me, I would go down "under the power." But that

day it was just Kathryn—with her hands on my jaw. I loved her too much to disappoint her. With a sigh of resignation, I fell backwards into the arms of the man behind me. As the man helped me to my feet Kathryn moved in again. "I give you the glory. I give you praise." But this time I simply could not. I just stepped back when she touched me.[2]

Yet, in a previous Kuhlman meeting, Jamie had experienced the undeniable presence of God:

To my knowledge, she never touched me. I do remember looking up, seeing the underside of the grand piano, and thinking how silly I must look . . . in front of seven thousand people. Then I was aware of the presence. A sort of euphoria swept over me, and I put my head back on the splintery wooden floor and just basked in the presence of God. . . . I lay there long after the other men had already taken their seats, preparing for the closing moments of the service. I finally crawled out from my cleft of the rock and took my chair, but I've never again doubted the slaying power of the Holy Spirit.

It's the ersatz "slayings," the manufactured ones, that invite derision. In the satirical religious magazine *The Wittenburg Door*, a reporter presents his view of what took place in a well-known evangelist's meeting:

It's pretty neat how it works. [He] prays along in a low, almost inaudible monotone with his hand in a sort of Spock-grip on their foreheads, and then . . . suddenly without warning shouts "Heal!" or "Jesus!" and gives their heads a hearty shove—a real hearty shove—backwards. If the yelling doesn't scare you into a faint, getting a hard shove on the head with your eyes closed oughta put you on the floor.[3]

Whether these specific allegations are true or not, they certainly give the healing ministry and the falling phenomenon a bad name.

Actually, the accusation of pushing may in some cases be unfounded. The most remarkable example I personally know about happened when I was praying with Judith several years before we married (in fact, before we were even thinking about marriage). She was with a few of her friends and one of them, Lynne Sunderland, told me that Judith had just been diagnosed as having a precancerous condition of the uterus and was threatened with a hysterectomy. Judith had been reluctant to bring this up, but she agreed to prayer, so we gathered around as she sat in her chair.

She closed her eyes and felt my hand upon her forehead. Then she felt her head being pushed back, so she resisted till her neck hurt. She was getting angry, so she opened her eyes to tell me to step back. But when she looked up there was no one in front of her; I was standing on the other side of the room.

The happy outcome: She was totally healed of the cancer. And now we have two beautiful children, Rachel and David! But that is another story.

Temptations of the Minister

If you find that people fall over when you pray for them, egotism and vanity are certainly temptations you will have to conquer. I remember that when I first saw people falling over as Kathryn Kuhlman prayed for them, my reaction was "*Wow!*" Most of us would like people to say that about our ministries. There is something in most of us, if we are honest, that likes to stand out from the crowd in some way; yet Jesus warned us not to stand on street corners to pray, hoping to be admired for our great religiosity. "Slaying people in the Spirit" is certainly a temptation to pride—one of the most spectacular manifestations the ministry can offer. It is dramatic, it is connected with *me*, it is visible. I need to work to counteract in my own spirit any desire to show off. I have to develop a sense of detachment about whether or not it happens at a given meeting—and certainly resist any effort on my part to make it happen.

Nor must I allow myself to feel inadequate when it doesn't happen (the flip side of pride). Suppose another minister and I are praying for two lines of people and nearly everyone in his line is falling, but nothing is happening in my line. Since the falling bodies can be seen by everyone, I am aware that people will be judging: "Pastor X has a lot of power in prayer, but this MacNutt seems pretty feeble in comparison. I think I'll go over to X." How would *you* react if that happened to you?

You know what the answer should be: Just go about your prayer, turn your heart and mind over to Jesus and forget about what people think.

The same thing is true of preaching: Preaching is meant to be a sharing of God's own Word. We try to make it that and become a clear pane of glass to let God's light through (knowing that, as in all things human, our views will be clouded by a certain amount of ignorance and prejudice).

Yet some preachers strive for dramatic effect and play excessively on people's emotions. Our sermons then become "Persuasion 101," more psychological manipulation than the Word of God. It is equivalent to pushing people over in a healing service!

In every area of our Christian ministry we need to be detached from our desire to make a reputation. The falling phenomenon is a good schooling ground: We can either watch it inflate our egos, or let it help us grow more centered on Jesus and less on ourselves.

The best attitude, then, is to desire that Jesus bless or heal a person through our prayer, but not specifically to desire that a person rest in the Spirit. If people do rest, it is a secondary effect, something that may help heal the sick and demonstrate God's power—not showcase our ministries. Since resting seems to be a condition conducive to healing, on the other hand, we can desire it in that sense—as an aid to healing rather than a primary goal.

What *other* people see as our priorities when we minister is important, too. We are a kind of teaching in ourselves. If they see us yearning for people to fall they will get an exaggerated notion of its importance. Some will then fall by reason of autosuggestion; others will get angry and come up in a resistant mood; still others who don't fall will feel guilty, because it seems to be so important. Such an exaggerated emphasis takes away the freedom of the congregation to respond to the Spirit, who blesses people in all kinds of ways.

Holy Contagion

While on the subject of the one who prays, let me offer an observation on one way in which this particular blessing is made increasingly available. When Judith and I pray in a church setting, we encourage the pastor to minister with us up front. Even in churches where resting in the Spirit has never happened before, people may start to fall over and rest in his or her line, too; and this continues to happen in that church after we leave. I'm not sure why this happens; all I know is that it does. The phenomenon seems to be contagious!

The Minister's Role

Some believe that falling is something we make happen; if we want a seemly, pure service, therefore, in which people are not distracted by showy phenomena, we can stop it if we wish. With the genuine article that is simply not so. If it is something the minister is somehow causing, then assuredly we should cease and desist. But if it is not something we are doing, the only way to stop it is to stop praying!—or to pray only briefly and without the laying on of hands.

And that means, so far as I can see, that many people will be deprived of a special encounter with Jesus. It's not that He can't minister to people without our intervention, or through silent prayer without the laying on of hands. But praying aloud for individuals, with the imposition of hands, is an ancient and effective form of intercession that I would hate to see the Church abandon because it occasionally has startling results!

Those of us who pray need to remind ourselves, too, that people's resting in our services is not a sign of holiness on our part. As Dr. John White observes:

Churches are slowly getting used to the fact that this or that Christian leader, who "was being tremendously used by God," was all along involved in secret sins of one sort or another. While the sin is upsetting, it is even more disturbing to us that "God continued to use" the person. (The fact is that the leader was not "being used by" God at all. If anything he was using God—or at least God's power. . . .)

. . . Results prove only that the power is real. The fact that the power of many delinquent healers comes from God lies in the fact that untold numbers of lives are redeemed through their ministry. God fulfills his own purposes. His loving heart is satisfied. But the results prove nothing about the character or holiness of the person who wields the power.[4]

As Jesus warned: "For false Christs and false prophets will appear and perform great signs and miracles to deceive even the elect—if that were possible" (Matthew 24:24).

When our hearts are in the right place, however, the very opposite of spiritual pride will be our reaction to the falling phenomenon. Instead of being tempted to self-satisfaction, we will be overwhelmed by a sense of our own littleness when we see, through no effort of our own, people begin to be healed as they rest in the Spirit. If we are guilty of no spiritual striving, if we are not inwardly using a kind of psychic force by desiring the person to go down, if we are not guilty of physically pushing, then our humility will grow.

We will see with absolute clarity that we are not doing this, but God is. As Mother Teresa says, we are pencils in the hand of God. Once I see that, how can I be proud?

12
Where and How Long?

One of the more mysterious elements of resting in the Spirit is that some *places* seem conducive to its happening while other sites block and prevent it. Then, too, the length of *time* that people rest varies widely, and I will try to suggest why. First . . .

The Place

Sometimes when we pray in a church service almost everyone falls; at other times maybe only one out of ten rests. Most of this, I believe, has to do with the receptivity of the group we are praying with.

But there also seems to be an element of blessing, or the lack of it, on certain places. Churches and rooms where many people have prayed seem to be likely, prepared sites for God's work. When I lived at Merton House in St. Louis, people came occasionally for prayer because they were "hearing" frightening voices; as soon as they walked in the door the voices ceased. The Holy Spirit was apparently shutting down the psychological forces or the demonic spirits, so that the afflicted persons would be open to healing.

Judith had similar experiences when she ran Christian Counseling Services in Clearwater, Florida. As soon as a client who was hallucinating walked into her office, the hallucinations stopped. It seems that when we spend a lot of time in prayer in a place, God comes to reside there in a very special way.

On the other hand, there seem to be some places that are, as it were, cursed. Our team will sometimes notice that a certain part of a particular church seems to be "cold." We can only guess the reason for this: Perhaps it is because some sin has been committed in that part of the building. The Catholic Church has recognized this for centuries: when a particularly heinous crime, such as murder, has been committed in a church, the local bishop will exorcise the building, as though an evil influence has established a "right" to abide there and will remain until it is cast out.

At the famous seminary of Maynooth in Ireland, for example, one room is permanently boarded up because a seminarian who lived there committed suicide and the next two seminarians assigned to the room suffered extraordinarily powerful temptations to kill themselves.

In short, there are certain places where God seems more free to move, others that are resistant to the power of God.

The most striking example of this in my own experience occurred when our team was praying for a large number of people one by one in a seminary in Honduras. Much healing was taking place, and many people were also resting in the Spirit. There was such a crowd of people, though, that it seemed wise to split our team. So I asked

Father Paul Schaaf to take part of the crowd to another room, *identical* to the one in which we were praying. After a short time Paul came back in and said there was a feeling of oppression in the other room and nothing was happening there. So his team rejoined us and we all prayed together again in the room where God's presence was manifest.

Duration

How long does this state of resting last? Several times I have seen it last as long as six hours. In one instance, in London, we had to rouse a woman so they could shut down the building where we were holding the meeting. At the other end of the spectrum (as with my own personal experience), we see people fall and get up quickly without much happening inside them.

A fascinating thing is that people who rest a long time usually think that they have been "out" for only a short time. At a Wimber conference, for instance, one woman estimated she had been on the floor for ten to fifteen minutes and was surprised to find that she had lain there for an hour and a half. With another, "It felt like just a few minutes, but when I came to I was still real groggy, and I'd been on the floor for four hours. Nearly everyone had gone home. I was real surprised."

If the resting lasts some little time, there is more opportunity for the Lord to work a profound change in the person's interior life. For this reason I now feel uncomfortable in those meetings where people are falling over like pins in a bowling alley, and then are quickly lifted to their feet, so that the next person can come up and occupy their space. It's as if the externals are emphasized with no understanding of their real purpose.

When someone does stay down a long time, it usually indicates that some kind of deep healing is going on and, for that reason, we tell ushers not to disturb the people who are resting or get them to their feet too quickly. From your own experience you know that you can't lie down on a floor for more than a few minutes without your body crying out in discomfort. Add to that a cold stone floor, such as many churches have, and you realize that something powerful must be going on inside the person to call attention away from bodily comfort. When the inner healing stops, the body's aches and pains become conscious and people get to their feet as soon as they can. We don't need to prod them into action.

The length of time that elapses while people rest, then, seems to allow God's healing presence to move deeply into their souls and transform their lives, as in the following incident:

> The Holy Spirit's power descended on Steven. He was uncertain what was happening, since his legs became unmovable while his body began to feel heavy, as though he were drugged. He closed his eyes. Bewildered, he found himself swaying. . . .
>
> By this time he was not sure whether he was asleep or awake, but sensed people gathering round him and praying. Then as he began to fall backward he was laid on a row of seats by the people around him. He felt ashamed, feeling he ought to get up since there were "so many things he ought to be doing for the Lord." Into his heart came the words *No, this is your time. Open your heart.*

He experienced a sensation as if he were melting into the chairs. He had no clear sense of time but was told he lay there about forty-five minutes. During that time Steven saw in his mind the Lord reach down to where he was lying and pluck his heart from his body, saying, *That's no good. You'll never do anything with that.* Then the Lord plucked His own heart from His chest and put it inside Steven's body, saying, *There! You can do something with that!*

Steven wept brokenly, his body shaking violently, and cried, "Lord, I love You so much—and I can't believe You love people as much as that!"

. . . He got up from the chair, still feeling the weight of the Lord's presence. When he began to move, "It was like slow-motion football." Feeling sure that the Lord's presence was "on him" for some purpose, he walked across to a hospital close by, and after eating lunch there, visited a couple of the patients, who were both healed as he laid his hands on them and prayed for them.[1]

These deep transformations are, of course, what we look for while people rest in the Spirit. To get statistics on this is difficult without extensive follow-up. As I have said, perhaps two out of three people raise their hands at the end of our conferences to indicate that they believe they have received a significant inner healing—and much of this takes place while resting in the Spirit.

For most people at our services the resting lasts only a minute or two. Perhaps one out of ten will rest for five minutes, and one out of a hundred for half an hour or more.

All this is important for us to understand, because what goes on in most large-scale healing crusades—the noise, the loud music, getting people quickly to their feet to accommodate the crowd flow can easily be a distraction, drawing the resting person's attention to the outside, rather than within where the Lord may wish to transform his life.

How Long Should You Pray?

As for the amount of time we spend praying with people I have found (maybe this is just for a few ministries like ours) that not much really happens of a deep order unless we pray for at least twenty seconds with each person who comes forward in a healing line. In most evangelistic services the prayers—if they are individual at all—have to be virtually instantaneous because of the large crowds. People at those services also tend to fall quickly and get up quickly. I know that remarkable healings take place at these meetings, but I don't believe that as many people are healed as might be if more time were available. Twenty seconds may, in fact, sound like a ridiculously short time, but multiplied by hundreds of people it makes a long evening. Those of us with experience know that praying for healing takes a lot out of you physically and emotionally; by 11 P.M. you need to stop!

The ideal would be to spend twenty minutes to an hour with each and every person, which is why we prefer whenever possible to work with teams. This gives the sufferer the individual prayer time needed to get at the cause of his distress. We need to pray for guidance and find out how best we can pray with people—and for how long. In short, to get out of the way and let Jesus do as He wishes.

13
Additional Patterns

Whenever there is a pattern there is usually a reason behind it, and if we can discover those reasons (God's purposes) we can better help people. Having seen thousands of people fall (and not fall), I offer these additional patterns I have observed.

Timing

Resting usually seems to happen after we have been praying for a while. If we are praying for people in a line, it is usually the third or fourth person who is the first to fall. Whatever this power is, it seems to increase after a period of prayer until it fills the entire room; at this point people sometimes begin to be overcome by the Spirit just as they stand there, without anyone touching them.

A spirit of praise, moreover, seems to increase the likelihood of resting. On occasion I have seen a group of priests overcome by the Spirit while praising God around an altar—with no prayers for individual needs whatsoever.

More people are usually overcome in the Spirit toward the end of a healing service than at the beginning. In a two-hour prayer session, the number of people who fall usually increases during the last fifteen minutes—just when those of us who are praying are most depleted and ready to stop. To me this is ample indication that the falling phenomenon owes nothing to human energy and effort. I know that it may sound pietistic, but it has always seemed to me that God is helping us out in a special way at the tail end of a service, just when we are physically at the end of our ropes.

Shaking

At our meetings most people rest quietly, but in Protestant revivals, as we have seen, many people trembled and shook. So, too, in our day, the shaking phenomenon occurs in John Wimber's conferences. At the 1986 Harrogate Conferences, for instance, some 26 percent of the people reported that their hands or arms shook. This seldom happens at our conferences unless an evil spirit is causing the agitation. Having great admiration for John Wimber and his ministry, we spent some time with him discussing this difference. Some of the possibilities we looked at:

> 1) At one time John was a Quaker pastor. The Quakers and the Shakers were originally given those names because they quaked and shook at their meetings under the power of the Holy Spirit. Perhaps this shaking phenomenon is part of John's spiritual heritage.

2) Perhaps there is more spiritual power at John's meetings. The poor human body just can't take it all and reacts as if touched by a jolt of electricity.

3) Our friend Art Thomson has suggested that different preachers have angels who help in their ministries. Perhaps a different group of angels travels with John!

4) Our ministry is largely one of inner healing through God's love and compassion. As we see it, people are filled with God's love up to the brim. When it gets to the top, as it were, the love overflows and they drift backward. John's ministry, on the other hand, emphasizes signs and wonders—demonstrations of God's power leading to evangelism. The Holy Spirit has a slightly different emphasis in Wimber's ministry than in ours—which is not to say that either is better; they are complementary.

Intensity

When people are resting in the Spirit, the physical component varies widely:

- Some are *able* to get up but just feel like resting and praying;

- Others are *unable* to get up and yet are fully aware of all that is going on around them;

- Still others are so caught up in an inward reality

that they are totally *unaware* of what is going on around them.

Speaking for myself I have never, when I have fallen, felt unable to get up; yet many of those we pray for (perhaps most) are—for a short while, anyway—immobilized physically. If they feel they ought to get up and go back to their pews, you will see them rise with difficulty and then stagger around as if drunk, making me think of Paul: "Do not get drunk on wine, which leads to debauchery. Instead, be filled with the Spirit" (Ephesians 5:18).

The intensity of inward experience varies widely, as we have seen—all the way from persons simply having a kind of rest (without much of anything going on inwardly) to a deep, transforming inner encounter. This encounter with the Spirit can increase in a person as you pray. It is almost as if a glass is being filled up: When the glass is full the person falls. This filling usually takes a bit of time, sometimes up to three or four minutes. So it seems to help if the person does not fall right away but waits until he or she has received as much of this life as possible and then stays down resting for a considerable time.

Again, though, the blessing is that interior encounter; whether the body falls or not is unimportant, as demonstrated in this letter received after a recent meeting:

> I really never thought I would have the "hysterical reaction" some before me in the chapel line had had—the falling back and the tears—because I am a non-hysterical type. However, when I asked you to pray I experienced a deep sense as of fire burning through me, tingling throughout my veins, trembling

as from too much pressure, and very weak knees. Actually, if I stayed a bit longer, I would also have fallen. I left you, dazed, staggering, tearful, and went to sit quietly, thankfully in the middle of the chapel. I stayed there until 11:45 P.M. and finally had to leave. I was praying throughout, mostly in wonder and thanks of God's great, immense gifts to me—especially Himself. . . . Today it is still with me, a sense of His being with me and my utter surrender to Him.

Other Observations

1) Sometimes people seem to fall in waves. Ten people in a row may go down, the next seven remain standing. Is it the power of suggestion? Is it a waxing and waning in the intensity of prayer?

2) Falling happens more frequently when a person asks prayer for himself or herself than when asking prayer for someone else.

3) Sometimes it happens at a distance, as if there were a force field of God's power. People may be waiting in line ten feet away and fall before they ever get near you for prayer.

4) Sometimes it happens to people who don't want it to happen. I will never forget a priest who attended one of the clergy retreats our team used to hold on Staten Island, New York. More than a hundred priests were present and this man had come to observe and scoff. On the last day he testified to the group that he was looking on, thinking it was all crazy, when suddenly he found himself on his back looking up. He was

a big man—250 pounds, I would guess—and as he lay there all he could think of was: *All these men are so pious, thinking their holy thoughts. But the only thing I feel like shouting is "Oh, [expletive deleted]!"*

5) Resting in the Spirit sometimes happens in private, too, when no group psychology is operative, and when the individual for whom we are praying is totally unfamiliar with the phenomenon.

6) While the person praying cannot induce any of these phenomena, the one being prayed for usually has a choice whether to resist or yield. Unless the power is very strong, he can usually successfully combat going down.

7) A few people—perhaps one out of twenty—fall forward instead of backward. This may indicate that the person is suffering from a deep sense of rejection and needs to be held. When a person starts leaning toward us we generally continue to pray and hold him or her upright in our arms. Often after two or three minutes the person falls back. Other times, if possible, we ask a team member to come and hold the person for a while. We have found that much inner healing comes in this way, without words; perhaps the person's inner child did not receive sufficient love from his or her mother or father. Afterward the person often says, "It wasn't as if you were holding me. After a while it was as if Jesus Himself came and held me until all my lonesomeness and depression went away."

These are a few of the patterns we have observed as Jesus heals His brothers and sisters while they rest in His presence.

14
Practical Decisions . . .
The Arrangements that
Work Best for Us

Why Not Sit Them Down?

Since it's the falling that attracts so much (often unfavorable) attention, why not sit people down when you pray for them?

This idea seems to make sense . . . until you try it. When you actually get to praying for a group of any size seated on chairs or in pews, you run into logistical problems. Actually, I usually do ask people to sit when we are one-on-one or in a small group setting. It's only in large groups that we pray for people standing, because of the problems we encounter with any other system. In a typical church it is awkward to set up, say, twenty chairs to accommodate 300 people waiting for prayer. And it is very difficult to maneuver around to pray for people in the pews. If you do set up chairs, it takes considerably more time to move people in and out of them than simply to pray for people who present themselves standing. It will turn a two-hour healing line into a three-hour one, which is a considerable time to ask people to wait, especially as this prayer ministry usually follows an hour and a half of singing and preaching.

A further problem, and a very real one, is what to do with someone who is overcome in the chair where he or she is sitting. Imagine the scene yourself! If you leave the person there, it takes a chair out of circulation. If you move him, it interrupts whatever the Spirit might be doing within the individual. Or suppose the person falls out of the chair. If the chairs are close, the resting person slumps over onto the next person, or falls to the floor in front of the chair, with legs twisted in a jumble. Someone then needs to straighten him out—in turn blocking access to the chair. (The same kinds of problems arise when people are overcome while kneeling at an altar rail.)

Another problem with ministering to someone in a chair: If people start to rest when they are sitting down, their heads tend to go backward and this puts a strain on the necks. Or they may start to rest and yet subliminally be so worried about toppling off the chair that their attention is distracted from the interior experience. The floor is a secure support where we've discovered people can let go and let God have His way!

Do You Mention It Before a Service?

Another recommendation is sometimes made that we say nothing about the falling phenomenon *before* a healing service. To do so, the argument goes, sets in motion the power of suggestion.

And it may be true: Suggestibility certainly is a factor with some people, as I have indicated. Experience has shown us, however, more compelling reasons on the side of making a brief explanation ahead of time.

Some kind of advance notice is needed, we have learned, because there are nearly always people present who have never seen someone fall. They are surprised, to say the least, when it occurs, and may even be frightened. So it is important to allay their fears.

Even if the sight doesn't frighten people, they may not understand the value of resting in the Spirit, especially in reference to inner healing. If they don't understand how it can be helpful, they are likely to fight it once it starts to happen to them. Sometimes you can just see the determination in a person not to let go—the grim set of the jaw, the squared shoulders; sometimes a person wobbles around in circles trying to avoid falling. This resistance may prevent some healing from taking place; the person is so set on staying up that he or she can't hear what God may be trying to communicate. At a time when we are hearing so much about addictions and codependency, which center on issues of control, I have often thought that being overcome in the Spirit might be a real help for those people who can't just "let go and let God."

The same wisdom applies when the phenomenon occurs to someone close to a first-time witness of these occurrences. Bystanders who do not understand what is going on will naturally worry about what is happening to their friends. Unless observers are acquainted with resting in the Spirit, they are likely to think that their friends have fainted and they may try to revive them. Concerned relatives will try to get a family member to sit up while he or she just wants to be left alone.

So, when I do give an explanation before a healing

service, I try first to give the purposes of resting in the Spirit as I see them, and then—to obviate the power of suggestion as much as possible—I ask people neither to *seek* the phenomenon nor to *fight* it. If we manufacture it, no one is helped. Indeed, trying to make it happen can actually block anything God might wish to do.

When people first began to fall under the power in my ministry, I not only shied away from speaking about it, but tried to keep it as inconspicuous as possible—mostly because of all the exhibitionism I had witnessed on TV. Whenever I noticed that someone was starting to fall, I would stop praying with that person, or else I would pray only with those who were sitting down.

But after a number of people shared with me the inner transformations they had experienced while resting, I came to the conclusion that my caution might actually be inhibiting the work of the Spirit. My own timidity and desire for respectability were getting in the way. I decided to let happen whatever was going to, and settled on a brief explanation ahead of time, keeping it as short as possible so as not to center attention upon externals.

Some suggest that we should wait until the falling happens before we talk about it; then, if it does, give an explanation. Again, this sounds good, and I have tried it, but it proves impractical. Picture the actual situation: You are praying with people one by one, and they start to drop. So you leave what you are doing, go back up to the lectern and give a five-minute explanation. In other words, you stop the prayer line to give a little talk. Your explanation is a very real interruption in the flow of the healing service. All things considered, we find it best to say something beforehand.

In my explanation, in addition to setting forth the

benefits of resting in the Spirit, I emphasize the following points:

1) Those who fall are no better than those who don't. Some people don't fall precisely because they are more spiritually mature and more accustomed to the presence and power of God.

2) Do not try in any way to make it happen.

3) Don't resist it, on the other hand, if you start falling.

4) Those of us doing the praying will try to be detached in our own desire as to whether or not it happens. Our intention is simply to be a channel to fill you with God's blessing.

5) Falling does not mean that something profound has taken place. We are not interested in the external—what happens to your bodies—but what happens inside your hearts. Some will be healed who do not fall. Some who fall will not be healed.

6) Some people may start to cry, as buried griefs are allowed to surface. If this happens to you don't stifle it, but let the emotion come out. We mention this because so many in our culture suppress their tears ("Grown men don't cry") and block their healing through a false sense of shame. We need to give people "permission" to let the tears flow.

Should We Provide "Catchers"?

The policy of stationing "catchers"—usually husky men—to stand behind people to cushion their fall gives rise to the same apprehension as speaking about the subject before it happens. Doesn't this procedure, too, send up a very definite signal that people are expected to fall? Create a psychological predisposition in susceptible people?

Is it necessary, anyway? Many people report that they fall "softly as a feather." Others maintain that no one ever gets hurt when overcome in the Spirit; you don't need catchers if you trust God. Indeed, I have seen people who should have been injured, the way they hit the ground, and yet were unbruised. But I have found that even if it were true that no one gets hurt, many people, due to the natural fear of falling, will fight any tendency to go over backward unless they have the human reassurance of someone standing behind them.

Even more important, I learned my lesson that occasionally a person may be hurt. In the early '70s, when resting in the Spirit was new to me, I was praying for a group of people during a conference in Arkansas. The room had a concrete floor, and I had just reached out my hand toward a woman who had come forward for a blessing. I don't think I even touched her when she went down and hit the back of her head with a horrendous cracking noise. Now, I had heard the proverb that no one is ever hurt at these times. Yet here she was, obviously injured; naturally, we all gathered 'round and started praying. After a while she smiled and got up, saying she would be fine.

But that night her roommate came knocking at my door saying that a lump was rising on the back of her friend's head and asking if she would be lacking in faith if she took her to a doctor. I encouraged her to do that immediately. She was taken to the emergency room where she was diagnosed as having a concussion and was immediately hospitalized.

The outcome of all this was happy. The woman, it turned out, had always wanted her husband to attend some spiritual event with her where she hoped he'd find a deeper relationship with God. He had always refused. But while she was in the hospital he visited her every day and there met a number of people attending the conference who also went to visit her every day; the result was that her husband was touched in the way she had always desired. She was released from the hospital at the very time the conference ended, her purpose accomplished!

More recently (1989) a federal jury has ordered evangelists Charles and Frances Hunter to pay $300,000 in damages to a 67-year-old woman who was hurt when she fell over backward during one of their healing services. Evelyn Kuykendall of Maxville, North Carolina, fractured her back and spent two months in the hospital following the accident.

The Hunters testified that Mrs. Kuykendall fell in a "peculiar way" and that their catchers could not intercept her fall. (The accident, interestingly, did not affect Mrs. Kuykendall's confidence in the Hunters' ministry; after the verdict was announced the three embraced.)[1]

In any event, I learned to be cautious and to ask for catchers to stand by any time I think that people might fall. In the seventeen years since that Arkansas conference, however, I have seen thousands of people rest in the Spirit, and I know of no one since then in our ministry who has been injured.

15
One Last Word

Writing this book has been a great help to me—not only clarifying my thoughts on this fascinating subject but deepening my insight into what Christianity is all about. It might seem that a book about people being slain by the Spirit concerns a somewhat peripheral—even superficial—topic, hardly at the center of what Jesus is all about. But a central message becomes increasingly clear as I spend time studying this mystifying phenomenon.

Let me try to explain. What is the overwhelming impression we gain from seeing or hearing about the external manifestations: bodies toppling over, some people unable to move, people being carried from the church when it is time to turn out the lights? Do we or do we not assign "catchers"? Some people crying, others laughing. The one word summing up everything that happens is *ridiculous.* As I mentioned earlier, it's like watching someone slip on a banana peel.

Is there any purpose behind all this ridiculous clown-ishness?

I believe that God (assuming that God is really in it) has

a very serious purpose behind it all. The issue is simply that we have followed the usual human inclination of paying lip service to God's sovereignty but have really taken over control of our lives and of God's Church; God wants to show, symbolically and dramatically, that He wants it back. "Give Me back My Church," he said to John Wimber. He is knocking the props out from under us. The more respectable, the more elegantly dressed, the more important we are, the sillier we look as we fall. A king with his crown or a mitered bishop looks more ridiculous when he falls, than does a poorly dressed migrant worker. In 2 Timothy 3:5 Paul tells us that a time will come when we maintain the form of religion but deny the real power of it. That's a constant human failing. I believe that people "falling under the power" has a prophetic impact: We become instantly aware that God's power is made manifest in our weakness. We are asked to let go of our controls; and we may not like that humbling fact at all. The great revivals, as we have seen, have often featured Spirit-empowered preaching accompanied by listeners falling, fainting, shouting and dropping to the ground as if felled by a giant cannon shot.

Yes, being felled by the Spirit looks slightly ridiculous, as we become aware that we are weak human beings in the presence of a mighty God, aware that we are merely the clowns of God face to face with the power of our Creator. In some sense I believe God is knocking us off our feet as a kind of prophetic action to demand that we relinquish control over our lives—and over the Church—to Him.

Remember Brother Tony who was immobilized in his

chair for two hours? Twenty years ago, as his glasses were slipping down his nose, Tony thought he understood what God was trying to get through to him. Today that same message to us is even more urgent:

"Without Me you can do nothing!"

Notes

Introduction

[1] Fr. Theodore Dobson, *The Falling Phenomenon* (Pecos, N.M.: Dove Publications, 1986), pp. 68–69.

[2] Cardinal Leon-Joseph Suenens, *Resting in the Spirit: A Controversial Phenomenon* (Dublin: Veritas Publications, 1987), pp. 73–74.

[3] Dr. John White, *When the Spirit Comes with Power* (Downers Grove, Ill.: InterVarsity Press, 1988), p. 137.

1 My Own Experience

[1] Cardinal Leon-Joseph Suenens, *Resting in the Spirit: A Controversial Phenomenon* (Dublin: Veritas Publications, 1987), p. 33.

[2] Cardinal Leon-Joseph Suenens, *Malines Document 2: Ecumenism and Charismatic Renewal* (Ann Arbor, Mich.: Servant Books, 1978), p. 66.

[3] As quoted in Johannes Jorgenson, *Saint Catherine of Siena*, translated by Ingeborg Lund (London: Longmans, Green and Co., 1938), p. 15.

2 What Happens When People Fall?

[1] This and the following excerpt are from *The Life of Teresa of Jesus*, translated by E. Allison Peers (Garden City, N.Y.: Image Books, 1960), pp. 196, 198.

[2] Dr. David Lewis, *Healing: Fiction, Fantasy or Fact* (London: Hodder & Stoughton, 1989), p. 192.

[3] Dr. John White, *When the Spirit Comes with Power* (Downers Grove, Ill.: InterVarsity Press, 1988), pp. 106–108.

[4] Lewis, pp. 184–185.

[5] This and the following excerpt are from White, pp. 197–198, 117.

[6] This and the following excerpt are from White, pp. 80–81.

3 Why Is It Helpful to Rest in the Spirit?

[1] Cardinal Leon-Joseph Suenens, *Resting in the Spirit: A Controversial Phenomenon* (Dublin: Veritas Publications, 1987), p. 22.

[2] Dr. David Lewis, *Healing: Fiction, Fantasy or Fact* (London: Hodder & Stoughton, 1989), p. 198.

[3] Bishop David Pytches, *Come, Holy Spirit* (London: Hodder & Stoughton, 1985), p. 153.

[4] Lewis, p. 191.

[5] Lewis, pp. 92–93. Although the man was fighting being slain in the Spirit, the other overpowering elements of the experience are akin to it.

[6] Rev. Benedict Haren, *Praying for Healing* (London: Darton, Longman & Todd, 1989), p. 70.

[7] Pytches, p. 153.

[8] A prayer that we use for protection is one we have adapted from Fr. Richard McAlear who has much experience and wisdom in the healing ministry:

> In the name of Jesus Christ, and by the power of His cross and blood, we bind up any evil spirits, forces and powers of earth, air, fire or water, of the netherworld and of nature. By the sword of the Spirit and in the authority of Jesus Christ let us be set free from any curses, hexes or spells, and let them be sent back

to those who sent them. We plead the protection of the shed blood of Jesus Christ on our meeting and command that any departing spirits leave quietly, without disturbance, and go straight to Jesus Christ for Him to dispose of as He sees fit.

[9] Dr. John White, *When the Spirit Comes with Power* (Downers Grove, Ill.: InterVarsity Press, 1988), pp. 217–218.

[10] Charles and Frances Hunter, *Since Jesus Passed By* (Van Nuys, Calif.: Time-Light Books, 1973), pp. 16–17.

[11] Teresa of Avila, *Interior Castle*, translated by E. Allison Peers (Garden City, N.Y.: Image Books, 1961), p. 184.

5 Do You Find It in the Bible?

[1] Cardinal Leon-Joseph Suenens, *Resting in the Spirit: A Controversial Phenomenon* (Dublin: Veritas Publications, 1987), p. 40.

[2] Dr. David Lewis, *Healing: Fiction, Fantasy or Fact* (London: Hodder & Stoughton, 1989), pp. 187–188.

6 Rapt in Ecstasy: The Catholic Tradition

[1] *The Life of Teresa of Jesus*, translated by E. Allison Peers (Garden City, N.Y.: Image Books, 1960), pp. 177–178.

[2] This and the three following excerpts are from *The Sermons and Conferences of John Tauler*, translated by the Very Rev. Walter Elliott (Washington, D.C.: Apostolic Mission House, a private printing, 1910), pp. 30–40. John Tauler is referred to as Master because he was a Master of Sacred Theology, an honorary title given in the Dominican Order.

[3] This and the following excerpt are from Paul Dudon, *St. Ignatius of Loyola*, translated by William Young (Milwaukee: Bruce Publishing, 1949), p. 114.

7 Spreading the Word: The Protestant Tradition

[1] Dr. John White, *When the Spirit Comes with Power* (Downers Grove, Ill.: InterVarsity Press, 1988), p. 45.

[2] Ronald Knox, *Enthusiasm* (New York: Oxford University Press, 1961), p. 535.

[3] Knox, p. 472.

[4] From John Wesley's *Journal*, entry date July 28, 1762.

[5] Wesley's *Journal*, September 8, 1784.

[6] Arnold A. Dallimore, *George Whitefield*, Vol. 1 (Westchester, Ill.: Crossway, 1980), p. 326.

[7] Wesley's *Journal*, June 5, 1772.

[8] Jonathan Edwards, *The Great Awakening*, edited by C. C. Goen (New Haven, Conn.: Yale University Press, 1972), p. 230.

[9] This and the following excerpt are from Jonathan Edwards, "Some letters relating to the Revival: to the Rev. Thomas Prince of Boston," p. 546.

[10] *Christian History*, Vol. VIII, No. 3, Issue 23, p. 23.

[11] Wesley's *Journal*, July 7, 1739.

[12] Dallimore, Vol. 2, pp. 392–393.

[13] White, p. 31.

[14] Marguerite Melcher, *The Shaker Adventure* (Princeton, N.J.: Princeton University Press, 1941), p. 14.

[15] Knox, p. 62.

[16] *Christian History*, p. 25.

[17] *Christian History*, p. 26.

[18] *Christian History*, p. 26.

[19] Charles Johnson, *The Frontier Camp Meeting* (Dallas: Southern Methodist University Press, 1955), pp. 64–65.

[20] Charles Finney, *Revival Fire* (Minneapolis: Bethany Fellowship, 1960), pp. 34–35.

[21] John Wimber, *Power Healing* (San Francisco: Harper & Row, 1987), pp. 259–260. From Appendix F, "Signs and Wonders in Sheffield," by Dr. David Lewis.

[22] This and the following two excerpts are from John Wimber, *Power Evangelism* (San Francisco: Harper & Row, 1986), pp. 24–27.

8 Objections

[1] Cardinal Leon-Joseph Suenens, *Malines Document 2: Ecumenism and Charismatic Renewal* (Ann Arbor, Mich.: Servant Books, 1978), p. 67.

[2] Dr. David Lewis, *Healing: Fiction, Fantasy or Fact* (London: Hodder & Stoughton, 1989), p. 176.

[3] Lewis, p. 174.

[4] Dr. John White, *When the Spirit Comes with Power* (Downers Grove, Ill.: InterVarsity Press, 1988), pp. 45–46.

[5] White, p. 50.

[6] White, pp. 81–82.

9 Who Falls and Who Doesn't?

[1] Dr. John White, *When the Spirit Comes with Power* (Downers Grove, Ill.: InterVarsity Press, 1988), p. 112.

11 The One Who Does the Praying

[1] James Randi, *The Faith Healers* (Buffalo: Prometheus Books, 1987), p. 238.

[2] This and the following excerpt are from Jamie Buckingham, *Daughter of Destiny* (Plainfield, N.J.: Logos, 1976), pp. 281, 232–233.

[3] Brad Bailey, "Robert Tilton," *The Wittenburg Door*, September–October 1989, p. 28.

[4] White, pp. 133–134.

12 Where and How Long?

[1] Dr. John White, *When the Spirit Comes with Power* (Downers Grove, Ill.: InterVarsity Press, 1988), pp. 15–16.

14 Practical Decisions

[1] *The Wittenburg Door*, January–February 1990, p. 39.

Reading List

To introduce people to elements of charismatic renewal, these are only a few, a very few, of the many fine books available on these topics.

Baptism of the Spirit

Bennett, Dennis. *Nine O'Clock in the Morning*. Bridge Publishing, S. Plainfield, N.J., 1970. This is Dennis Bennett's personal story of how he experienced the baptism of the Holy Spirit as an Episcopal pastor in Van Nuys, California.

Bennett, Dennis and Rita. *The Holy Spirit and You*. Bridge Publishing, S. Plainfield, N.J., 1971. This is an explanation of what the renewal of the Holy Spirit is all about.

Bennett, Dennis. *How to Pray for the Release of the Holy Spirit*. Bridge Publishing, S. Plainfield, N.J., 1985.

The Gift of Tongues

Sherrill, John. *They Speak with Other Tongues*. Chosen Books, Old Tappan, N.J., 1964 and 1985. This easy-to-read book is the classic on this subject.

Healing

Dobson, Theodore. *Inner Healing: God's Great Assurance.* Paulist Press, Mahwah, N.J., 1978.

Lewis, Dr. David. *Healing: Fiction, Fantasy or Fact.* Hodder & Stoughton, London, 1989. A comprehensive analysis of the varied spiritual phenomena at John Wimber's Harrogate (England) Conference, based on 1,890 questionnaires.

Linn, Dennis and Matthew. *Healing Life's Hurts.* Paulist Press, Mahwah, N.J., 1978.

MacNutt, Francis. *Healing* (Protestant edition). Creation House, Lake Mary, Fla., 1988.

MacNutt, Francis. *Healing* (Catholic edition). Image Books, New York, 1990. A basic overview of the whole subject of praying for healing that has sold nearly a million copies since first coming out in 1974 (Ave Maria Press).

MacNutt, Francis. *Power to Heal.* Ave Maria Press, Notre Dame, Ind., 1977. A follow-up to *Healing,* this book shares what experience has taught us about the healing ministry (such as the need for "soaking prayer").

MacNutt, Francis. *The Prayer that Heals.* Ave Maria Press, Notre Dame, Ind., 1981. A small, practical book showing how to pray for healing in the family.

Sandford, John and Paula. *The Transformation of the Inner Man.* Victory House, Inc., Tulsa, 1982.

Tapscott, Betty. *Inner Healing Through Healing of Memories.* Hunter Books, Kingwood, Tex., 1975.

Wagner, Peter. *How to Have a Healing Ministry without Making Your Church Sick.* Regal Books, Ventura, Calif., 1988. Written for evangelicals, a persuasive case for introducing the healing ministry into the church.